The Early Cl

–a taster

Dr Richard Alderson

DayOne

Copyright © Day One Publications 1997
First printed 1997

Scripture quotations are from The King James Version

ISBN 0 902 548 77 8

Published by Day One Publications
6 Sherman Road, Bromley, Kent BR1 3JH

Designed by Steve Devane and printed by Clifford Frost Ltd, Wimbledon SW19 2SE

The Early Christians
–a taster

God's perfect timing

S ince the God of the Bible is the Sovereign Lord of history, we are not
surprised to learn that He had so ordered events that the Christian
Gospel began to be preached just at the time when the situation was
most favourable to its reception and spread (Galatians 4:4). This is true
from every standpoint – political, cultural, religious and moral.

Politically, the civilised world had been united under Roman rule, an
empire of 36 provinces, stretching from southern Britain to Armenia. A
powerful centralized government in Rome had eliminated all national
barriers. Universal peace, the Pax Romana, reigned virtually unbroken
until the end of the second century. A superb network of roads, straight as
a die, radiated from the Roman Forum to the Empire's furthest bounds.
(There were 5,000 miles in Britain alone.) Roman power had also swept
the Mediterranean clear of pirates. This meant that travel by both land
and sea was safe and reliable, and Christians readily availed themselves of
this opportunity to take the Gospel to many parts of the Empire.

Then there was the cultural unity resulting from the use of the Greek
language, carried far and wide by Alexander the Great's victorious
armies. This clearly represented an inestimable advantage to Christian
preachers, who could count on being understood almost everywhere
they went. It is of interest that the Jews in Jerusalem obviously expected
Paul to address them in Greek, not in Hebrew (Acts 21:40-22:2). And it
was the Septuagint, the Greek translation of the Old Testament, which
was in common use among the Jews of the Dispersion.

Religiously, it was this Dispersion which provided a bridgehead for the
Gospel. It is estimated that there were perhaps as many as five million Jews
very widely dispersed within the confines of the Roman Empire with its 70-
odd million souls. 'Already,' says the geographer Strabo, 'a Jewish population has entered every city, and it is not easy to find a place in the habitable
world which has not received this race, and is not possessed by it'.

Wherever they went, the Jews naturally established their synagogues.
And it was these centres of revealed religion which attracted the so-
called 'God-fearers'. These were people who were seeking spiritual

reality and an escape from the empty ritual of the heathen cults, to say nothing of their gross immoralities. (One thinks of the temple of Venus in Corinth with its 1,000-odd priestess-prostitutes.)

The synagogues became ready-made preaching centres where both Jew and God-fearing Gentile could hear Christian preaching from the Apostles and others. And it was the proselytes to Judaism who most readily embraced the new Gospel of hope, as we see in the case of Philippi and Thessalonica (Acts 16:14; 17:4). They had found the Messiah of the Old Testament – or rather had been found by Him.

Morally, the classical world had sunk to the abysmal level depicted in such passages as the second half of Romans chapter one. 'Everything is full of iniquity and vice,' writes Seneca. 'Daily the lust of sin increases; daily the sense of shame diminishes. Casting away all regard for what is good and honourable, pleasure runs riot without restraint'. Lucian saw Rome as the epitome of all avarice, pomp, flattery, hedonism, gluttony, carousals, lewdness, sorcery and lying. G.P. Fisher writes of 'a profligacy which probably has had no parallel, before or since, in the annals of the race'. Gibbon is therefore fully justified in asserting that 'Society was a rotting, aimless chaos of sensuality.'

As we shall see, there was a pleasure mania, with obscene plays and sadistic gladiatorial contests much in demand. Tertullian wrote of 'the maddening circus, the bloodthirsty arena, and the lascivious theatre'. Into this scene there irrupted the incomparable Christian ethic, exemplified in lives transformed by the wonder-working power of God. Many traced their conversion to observing such a life-changing agency at work. Justin Martyr expresses this miraculous change very beautifully in his First Apology: 'We who formerly delighted in fornication now strive for purity. We who used magical arts have dedicated ourselves to the good and eternal God. We who loved the acquisition of wealth more than all else now bring what we have into a common stock, and give to everyone in need. We who hated and destroyed one another and on account of their different manners would not receive into our houses men of a different tribe now since the coming of Christ live familiarly with them. We pray for our enemies, we endeavour to persuade those who hate us unjustly to live conformably to the beautiful precepts of Christ, to the end that they may become partakers with us of the same joyful hope of a reward from God, the Ruler of all.'

The Church and Society

It is difficult for those who live in our modern secular society to envisage the world in which the early Christians' lot was cast. Theirs was a world saturated with paganism and where pagan allusions met them at every turn. This was true from state affairs down to the trivia of everyday life. The Roman Senate always met in a place consecrated to some pagan deity and began its deliberations only after each Senator had duly offered wine on the altar. Solemn sacrifices to the gods marked the advent of peace or war. Public games and spectacles were celebrated in honour of some god or other.

In the home, there were pagan designs on furniture, ornaments, utensils and clothing alike. The hearth was guarded by the penates, the family's ancestral gods. Strange as it may seem to us, there was one god of the threshold and another of the door – even a goddess of the hinges! Births, marriages and deaths each boasted their presiding divinity. Here again we meet this extraordinary profusion of gods and goddesses. While one presided over the birth of a child, another undertook its nursing. The help of a third was besought on the ninth day, when the child was named. One goddess would superintend its weaning; another taught it to walk. Further division of labour meant that while one deity was responsible at the lisping stage, another took over when it came to talking.

Travel by land and sea came under the aegis of the relevant divinity. Soldiers, merchants, the childless, the blind – all were catered for. The list is endless – which occasioned Tertullian's jibe, 'Even the brothels and cookshops and prisons have their gods!' On festive days, garlands of flowers on the head and laurel branches on doors all carried superstitious overtones of some kind. Everyday idiom bristled with pagan allusions. Even a sneeze brought the response 'Jupiter bless you!'

It was against this background that the early church sought to discover what our Lord meant when He said that though Christians were 'in the world', they were not 'of the world'. In her attempt to maintain this delicate balance, the church has often swung violently from one extreme to the other – from the Scylla of monasticism and exclusivism on the one hand to the Charybdis of 'religionless Christianity' on the other.

How did the early Church face the dilemma? She did so by asserting that while she must of necessity avoid sinful practices (like abortion and the gladiatorial show), she nevertheless played her part in public life. Tertullian (c.160-230) indicated the extent of Christian involvement: 'We live in the world with you. We do not forsake forum ... or bath ... or workshop, or inn, or market, or any other place of commerce. We sail with you, fight with you, farm with you ... We do not go to your feasts but we patronise your industries. We do not buy laurel crowns but we buy flowers. We do not buy incense for temples but we do for burial. We do not contribute to the temples but we give more for alms than you do. We improve business in that we do not defraud.'

As Tertullian hinted, there were certain limits to a Christian's participation in public life, however antisocial such scruples might appear to his pagan contemporaries. While a Christian might be a sculptor, he would fight shy of making idols. He would not gild idols, though he would conscientiously gild other objets d'art. He would polish most articles, but not sacrificial knives. He might work in bone, but he certainly wouldn't cut bone tickets for the arena. Teaching was a problem, because of the need to teach classical myths. Work in hospitals raised the spectre of the patronage of Aesculapius. Politics seemed to raise insuperable barriers. A Christian might be a civil servant – if he could avoid the taint of idolatry and the need to take life. He certainly could not be an actor, or a gladiator, or a charioteer, or a magician, or an astrologer or a juggler. Church membership was automatically refused to the openly immoral, such as panders and prostitutes.

It was this scrupulosity which brought down on the head of the early church the charge of social irresponsibility. Tacitus accused Christians of 'hatred of the human race'. Celsus, in a scathing satire, averred that if everyone behaved like Christians, the empire would be overrun by barbarians.

A mere glance at the history of the early church is sufficient answer to these cheap jibes. Her social conscience was already evident in the Book of Acts, where assets were sold to help those in need, deacons appointed to tackle material problems, and contributions made for the poor.

Later history confirmed this trend. Justin (c.100-c.165) wrote: 'We who once took pleasure in means of increasing our wealth and property now bring what we have into a common fund and share with everyone in need'. Aristides added: 'He who has gives to him who has not, without grudging, and when they see a stranger they bring him to their dwellings and rejoice over him as a true brother.' The redoubtable Tertullian went further and carried his apologetic into the enemy camp: 'Our charity dispenses more in the streets than your religion in all the temples.' He roundly charged pagans with giving only the junk they had finished with.

The early church established funds to meet a variety of needs. Widows were maintained – 3,000 by the Church of Antioch alone in the time of Chrysostom (347-407). Captives were ransomed. The Church in Carthage once gave £1,000 for this purpose. Ambrose (c.339-397) redeemed prisoners from the Goths with money realised from the sale of Church vessels. 'Better clothe the living temples of Christ than adorn the temples of stone' was Jerome's pertinent comment. Acacius, Bishop of Amida, followed suit. 'God has no need of plates and dishes,' he remarked, as he sold Church treasures to ransom captives. In addition, orphans were rescued from destitution and the clutches of unscrupulous men; martyrs' families were provided for; and hostels were run for the benefit of travellers.

Some pagan writers frankly granted the fact of Christian philanthropy. They were astonished by the contrast with their own theory and practice. Plato had taught them the moral excellence of allowing the poor to die, since it shortened their misery! Lucian, in a patently satirical work, was genuinely surprised by Christian concern for others. 'It is incredible,' he wrote, 'to see the ardour with which the people of that religion help each other in their wants. They spare nothing.' He noted their 'untiring solicitude and devotion' as they visited a prisoner and brought him meals.

Medical work was another area of Christian social concern. The classic account of this concerns Christians' selfless devotion to the victims of the third-century epidemic in Alexandria. Regardless of the danger, they tended the sick in the name of Christ. In fearlessly handling the dead and dying, they themselves contracted the dread plague. Labouring with 'great piety and strong faith', they finally succumbed and so 'departed this life serenely happy'. It all stood in stark contrast to the selfishness and panic of the unbelievers, who heartlessly abandoned their nearest and dearest in a vain attempt to avoid infection themselves.

Politics

As regards politics, early Christians generally took their attitude to the state from such passages as Romans 13:1-5. The powers-that-be were ordained of God and were therefore to be obeyed. Eastern writers saw state and church as joint agents under God for man's salvation. The state was 'the power that restraineth' of II Thessalonians 2, God's instrument for keeping sin in bounds. 'Since man,' wrote Irenaeus (c.140-c.202), 'in his departure from God, reached such a pitch of fury that he regarded his own brother as an enemy and engaged in all kinds of restless conduct without fear, God imposed upon man the fear of man.' The Roman Empire fulfilled its divine mission by sweeping the Mediterranean clear of pirates and the land of bandits, so facilitating the church's task of evangelism.

This did not mean that Christians readily entered politics. Origen (184-253), while conceding that the state served God's purpose, thought that it was ordained for non-Christians. Its use of force rather than love marked it out as sub-Christian. (He compared it to a chain gang, which did good work, though composed of criminals!) No Christian would dream of taking political office. He was called to the higher service of prayer. Tertullian too agreed that 'nothing is more alien to Christians than politics'. But he insisted that Christians were loyal citizens.

It was the Emperor's claim to deity which caused the trouble. Any Emperor who made such a claim – one thinks of Diocletian – ipso facto proclaimed himself 'the man of sin' of II Thessalonians 2, the abomination of desolation, the Anti-Christ. Loyal Christian subjects had to draw the line at such patent blasphemy. A government that restrained evil they would gladly obey; an emperor who arrogated to himself divine honours they would resist to the death.

But what of a persecuting government? This raised acutely the problem of obedience. When secular Rome persecuted, she looked suspiciously like the Whore of Revelation, drunk with the blood of saints. In such cases, Christians normally invoked Acts 5:29. It was better to obey God rather than men. This did not mean, however, that the Christian had the right to revolt. God would deal with recalcitrant governments. Hippolytus (c.170-235) rated sedition with fornication and astrology – activities which excluded from baptism. Non-Christians, however, were required to act, and when the Goths invaded the empire during the Decian persecution, Commodianus promptly wrote a poem welcoming them.

Pacifism

This must not be construed as implying that all Christians before Constantine were pacifists. There were Christians in the Roman Army. One thinks, for example, of the Thundering Legion in the time of Marcus Aurelius (reigned 161-180). At least six graves of Christian soldiers date from before Constantine – admittedly a very small number. Most Christians probably were pacifists. But Christian writers had difficulty defending their pacifism biblically. The Old Testament wars constituted a problem. These were usually explained either as belonging to an outdated dispensation or simply as allegories. Marcion went further. Like his modern heretical counterparts, he rejected the Old Testament completely as immoral. He contrasted Joshua (he meant Aaron and Hur!) holding up Moses' arms for slaughter with the Jesus of the New Testament holding out His arms to save. Origen (184-253) cut the Gordian Knot by asserting that the Old Testament wars were not real wars, just pictures of God's war with sin.

The New Testament also posed difficulties. It spoke, for example, of Christian centurions. Some writers therefore sought to resolve the problem by drawing a distinction between being in the army (an acceptable vocation) and actually killing (a 'mortal sin', so called). This was not an academic distinction. Roman soldiers might spend a lifetime in the army and never see war. They might spend their time mending roads, policing the streets, fighting fires and the like.

Tertullian took up an uncompromisingly pacifist position. 'There can be no agreement between the human and divine sacramentum, the standard of Christ and the devil, the camp of light and the camp of darkness. A Christian cannot serve two masters. People ask whether a baptized Christian can become a soldier, or whether a soldier may be admitted to the faith... One might suggest in jest that Moses carried a rod and Aaron wore a buckle, John had a leather belt, Joshua led an army, and Peter made war. But you tell me how Peter could have served in war, indeed even in peacetime, without a sword? Even if soldiers did come to John, and the centurion did believe, the Lord Himself unbelted every soldier when He took the sword from Peter.'

Origen argued for Christian exemption from military service. Not even the Emperor could make Christians fight They would form an 'army of piety' – prayer warriors supporting the Government's efforts by intercession.

Any Christian in the Army certainly faced grave problems, not simply that of taking life. He would have to attend pagan sacrifices, perhaps even offer sacrifice; and he would wear the objectionable lead seal with its pagan symbol. Rejection of these elements sometimes led to martyrdom. The story is told of Marcellus, a Christian centurion in Tangiers. Incensed at the paganism surrounding Maximian's birthday celebrations, he threw away his belt and stick, crying: 'I am a soldier of Jesus Christ, the eternal King. I have done with fighting for your emperors. I despise the worship of deaf and dumb gods of wood and stone. If the terms of service are such that one is bound to sacrifice to gods and emperors, then I refuse to be a soldier!'

The prefect remonstrated with him: 'How did you come to be so mad as to renounce your oath and speak like that?'

To that there was but one answer: 'There is no madness in those who serve the Lord.'

Undaunted and unembittered by the sentence of death, Marcellus simply said to his judge, 'God bless you!' It was, as the chronicler added, 'the proper way for a Christian to take leave of this world.'

Christian soldiers were naturally offended by the periodic bacchanalia which they sometimes witnessed. The winter solstice provided the opportunity for one such orgy. It was the feast of Saturn, now supplanted by Christmas. Soldiers would then elect one of their own number 'King'. After thirty days' carousal in the robes of Saturn, the 'King' would be sacrificed. A Christian, Dasius, was elected to this office, but steadfastly refused it. 'It is better,' he said, 'for me to be a sacrifice of my own free decision for our Lord Jesus Christ, than to be sacrificed for your idol Saturn.'

The Governor tried persuasion: 'Pray to the emblems of our lords the emperors, who maintain peace and give us our pay, and day by day in all things consider our good.'

'I repeat. I am a Christian and my war-lord is no emperor of flesh and blood, but the Emperor of Heaven. I am paid and fed by Him and His ineffable generosity makes me rich.'

'Fall down, Dasius, before the sacred images of our emperors, which even the barbarian tribes know and serve.'

'I owe allegiance to none save one, undefiled and eternal God, who will arm me with the strength to overcome and destroy speedily the raging of the Devil.'

Under sentence of death, he spurned last-minute efforts to induce him to offer incense to the Emperor. Seizing the incense vessel, 'he scattered the incense to the winds, trampled on the shameful and sacri-legious images of the blasphemous emperors and made the battle sign of the adorable cross of Christ on his brow, through whose power he stood firm against the tyrants.'

The case of Maximilian of Theveste is of interest because he was one of the few actually pressed into service by the powers-that-be.

'Put on the uniform,' said the governor.

'I cannot become a soldier. I cannot commit blasphemy. I am a Christian.'

The governor tried to hang the lead seal round Maximilian's neck, but he refused.

'Be a soldier or you die.'

'Strike off my head. I am no soldier of this world, but a soldier of God.'

'Be a soldier and accept the token.'

'I will not take this sign. I am already signed with the sign of my God,

Jesus Christ.'

'I will send you speedily to your Christ.'

'I wish you would do it at once.'

'Put on the token.'

'I will not put on the sign of this world and if you put it on me, I shall tear if off, for it has no meaning for me. I am a Christian and may not wear this piece of lead, now that the saving sign of my Lord Jesus Christ has come, the Son of the Living God, of whom you refuse to hear, who has suffered for our salvation, whom God gave for our sins. All we who are called Christians serve Him and follow Him, as the Prince of life and the Giver of salvation.'

'Let it be put on or you are a lost man.'

'I will not be lost. My name is written with my Lord.'

'Think how young you are, and become a soldier. It suits a young man.'

When Maximilian refused, the governor tried a different argument:

'In the holy service of our Lords Diocletian and Maximian, Christian soldiers also perform their service.'

'They must know for themselves what is right. I am a Christian and I cannot do anything blasphemous.'

'What blasphemies do soldiers have to perform?'

'You know yourself what they have to do.'

So the tyrant's sword despatched Maximilian to the presence of the Lord he had so dauntlessly refused to deny.

Slavery

Slavery was another social problem with which Christians were faced. Roman society was characterized by a relatively rigid class system: senator, citizen, freedman and – at the bottom – the unfortunate slave. Slaves, usually prisoners-of-war, were regarded by their masters as nothing but 'animated tools'. 'Tools,' wrote Varro, 'are of three kinds: vocal, including slaves; semi-vocal, for example oxen; and dumb, for instance ploughs.' Slaves were not regarded as human beings, and therefore had no rights, no will of their own, and no property. Like oxen or ploughs, they could be bought and sold, lent, given or bequeathed at will. Branded and marked, they could be tortured, maimed, flogged and crucified for the slightest offence at their master's caprice. Some were despatched to the mines – or the brothels. Those on farms often worked in chains, feeding at the cattle troughs and sleeping in the stalls. On death, their bodies were thrown unceremoniously into pits with dead animals.

The slave system eroded the whole life of the ancient world – politically, economically and morally. The subjugated, unprivileged slave class bore the heat and burden of the day while their leisured masters gave free rein to their passions. The idle aristocrat spent his time between the unfortunate slave women in the house and the sadistic displays in the amphitheatre, where vast numbers of slaves made possible endless fights with man and beast.

In stark contrast with that sordid picture stands the glorious liberty made possible in Christ Jesus. In the church of God there was 'neither bond nor free'. Onesimus the slave became a 'brother beloved' (Philemon 16). The early Fathers reflected the same high view. Aristides wrote: 'Slaves, male and female, are encouraged to be instructed in Christianity on account of the love their masters have for them. When this happens, they are called brethren, without any distinction.' Lactantius agreed: 'Slaves are not slaves to us. We deem them brothers after the Spirit, in religion fellow-servants.' Euelpistes, himself a slave in the imperial household, told his judge: 'I am a slave of the Emperor, but I am also a Christian and have received liberty from Jesus Christ; by His grace I have the same hope as my brethren.'

It is significant that the inscription 'slave', so common on heathen graves, does not once appear in the catacombs. From the start, office in the church was open to slaves. Callistus, an ex-slave, became Bishop of Rome.

Converted slaves shared equally in the trials of their fellow-Christians of higher station. Blandina, a teenage slave, suffered martyrdom in Lyons with her mistress; Felicitas went hand-in-hand with the high-born Perpetua to face a wild cow in the arena at Carthage.

It may be asked whether early Christians did more than mitigate the evils of slavery. The answer is that they were encouraged to free slaves. Congregations set up special funds to purchase their freedom. After manumission (freedom), the Christian master would take his freedman to a service, where the document of emancipation was read. The ex-slave was then embraced by the congregation as a free brother. We read of one rich Christian who, on the day of his baptism, freed 1,250 slaves. Nor was this an isolated case.

Marriage

We turn now to the Christian attitude to women and marriage. It is a commonplace that pagan culture at the time of Christ degraded women and debased marriage. A woman was regarded more as a chattel than a person. Plutarch tells us that her rights and interests were totally subordinated to those of her husband. She had no friends or gods but his.

It was a permissive age. Even eminent moralists like Cicero and Cato were known to be adulterers. Divorce was the order of the day. Seneca notes that in Nero's reign women measured their years by husbands, not consuls. Martial tells of one woman who married ten husbands in one month, while Jerome later speaks of one woman married 23 times. They were no doubt exaggerating, but the marital laxity of the period lies beyond dispute. Fidelity was ridiculed. Wife-swapping and seduction were regarded as a huge joke.

It was the glory of Christianity that it elevated the status of women and stressed the sanctity of the marriage bond. St. Paul could give marriage no higher honour than to employ it as a type of the union between Christ and His church. Many early Christian writers held this biblical view of marriage. So Tertullian contended vigorously (as was his wont) for monogamy. If God had intended polygamy, He would have used more than one of Adam's ribs! God had permitted polygamy to the patriarchs only because the world was underpopulated.

The Fathers generally adduced two purposes of marriage – children and mutual spiritual support. The primary reason in their view was the procreation and nurture of children. This stood in marked contrast to the attitude of many pagans. 'We destroy monstrous offspring,' declared Seneca. 'If they are born delicate or deformed, we drown them. It is not passion but reason that separates the useless from the healthy.' Less fortunate were the many healthy infants who were exposed to die of cold or hunger – or to be eaten by dogs.

If Christians did not want children, they abstained from sex. Contraception was universally frowned on in the church. This matter received prominence under Callistus, when certain noblewomen were loath to bear children to slaves, since any offspring automatically took slave status.

The second purpose of marriage was mutual spiritual comfort, and in a passage of rare beauty Tertullian depicts this for us. 'How can I paint the happiness of a marriage that the church cements, the celebration of communion confirms, the benediction seals, news of which is carried back by the angels and ratified by the Father? What a union! Two believers sharing one hope, one rule of life and one service! They are brother and sister, two fellow-servants, one in flesh and spirit. They pray together, fast together, teach, exhort and support each other. They go together to the church of God and to the Lord's table. They share each other's tribulations, persecutions and revival. Neither hides anything from the other, shuns or is burdensome to the other. They delight to visit the sick, help the needy, give alms freely. In psalms and hymns they vie with each other in praising God. Christ rejoices when He sees and hears such things. He is with them and sends them His own peace.'

Tertullian then depicts the evils of a mixed marriage. 'How can a woman serve two masters, the Lord and a husband – let alone a heathen husband? If there is a meeting to attend, he gives her an appointment for the baths. If there are fasts to be kept, he chooses the day for a dinner party. If she has a charitable errand, never is household work more in the way. For who would let his wife go round street by street to other men's houses, and indeed to all the poor cottages, to visit the brethren? Who will willingly let her be taken from his side for nocturnal meetings, and especially for the all-night service at Easter? Who will let her go without suspicion of his own to that Lord's Supper which they defame? Who will let her creep into a prison to kiss a martyr's bonds, or even to give the kiss of peace to one of the brethren? God's handmaid is persecuted with the odour of incense at all the festivals of the demons, and on every day of public rejoicing. She will dine with her husband in clubs, often in taverns; and sometimes she will minister to the unjust –the very men she was to judge hereafter.'

Unfortunately, not all the Fathers held a biblical view of marriage. Second marriages were discouraged or even condemned as 'a respectable form of adultery'. More extreme teachers condemned marriage altogether as unspiritual. Tatian dubbed it 'defilement' and 'fornication'. Where most Christians, following the Apostle Paul, saw celibacy, like marriage, as a gift of God, the heretic Marcion exalted it above marriage and imposed it on his followers. In later years Tertullian became much more rigorous. He argued against marriage as a 'voluptuous disgrace', regarded wives as encumbrances in the Christian warfare, and finally asserted that, in this new dispensation of the Spirit, Christians should follow Christ's example and remain celibate. This imbalance was of course later reflected in monasticism. Jerome contrasted the gold and silver of celibacy with the earthenware of marriage. 'The 30-fold increase of Scripture,' he wrote, 'refers to marriage; 60-fold to widowhood; but 100-fold to virginity. Marriage replenishes earth but virginity heaven.' Happily, this ran quite counter to the generally accepted view.

Luxury

The Fathers were unanimous in their aversion to luxury in any shape or form. They followed the Cynics in making utility the sole criterion. Clement (c.150-c.215) stood alone in his defence of wealth. But he recognised how dangerous it was – 'like a snake that will bite unless we know how to take it by the tail.' The well-to-do Christian was to use his wealth aright – for charitable purposes. Clement had been nauseated by the unashamed luxury of the East – expensive jewellery and dress, ornate baths, sumptuous banquets, glittering chariots and litters. Leisured ladies of substance were squandering wealth and affection on monkeys, peacocks and Maltese dogs. (One could think of modern counterparts!) It was for these abuses that he reserved his severest strictures.

Pursuing his case for utility, Clement argued that a knife didn't need silver studs and an ivory handle to cut well; an earthenware lamp worked just as well as a gold one; a bed didn't need to be made of ivory; and goatskins served as well as colourful counterpanes. In all this we had the example of 'the lowly-minded God and Lord of the Universe', who had used the meanest utensils in His days on earth.

Cyprian (c.200-258) argued from the carking care produced by possessions and urged the culture of the soul. He pictured the bloated plutocrat nervously drinking from his jewelled goblet and spending sleepless nights on a downy bed, enslaved by his possessions and fearful of burglars. How much better to turn from houses encrusted with gold which must soon tarnish, so that we may devote ourselves to embellishing the soul, the temple of God's Spirit, with a beauty that can never fade away.

With preparation for martyrdom in mind, Tertullian warned against pampering the body. How would the wrist with a delicate bracelet stand a chain? Or the bejewelled neck the executioner's axe? How would the ornamented leg fare under the screw? We must cast away earthly jewellery if we desire heavenly. Comeliness is to be the godly garment of the soul. 'Be arrayed in the ornaments of the apostles and prophets, drawing your whiteness from simplicity, your ruddy hue from modesty, painting your eyes with bashfulness, your mouth with silence, implanting in your ears the Word of God, fitting on your neck the yoke of Christ. Clothe yourself with the silk of uprightness, the fine linen of holiness, the purple of modesty, and you shall have God Himself for your lover and spouse.'

Many of the Fathers reserved their most biting satire for cosmetics and hair-dos. 'What business,' asked Jerome (340-420), 'have rouge and paint on a Christian cheek? Who can weep for her sins when her tears wash bare furrows on her skin? With what trust can faces be lifted to heaven which the Maker cannot recognise as His workmanship?' Cyprian warned that God might not recognise them at the resurrection! Clement reminded them that 'they cannot with their bought and painted beauty avoid wrinkles or evade death.' Hair was not to be dyed, since 'thou canst not make one hair white or black.' Tertullian, true to form, inveighs against the squandering of time in the boudoir – witness those great masses of hair dyed auburn (then the 'in' colour). In the unbecoming search for new styles, the poor hair was allowed no rest –

now bound, now loosed; now raised, now flat. Some had it curled, others let it lie loose and flying. Then there were those wigs, built up with pads and rolls, 'the slough perhaps of some guilty wretch bound for hell'. Of what value was all that to the soul? Could women so tricked out expect the angels to carry them to meet Christ in the air on the Judgement Day?

Clothes were not to be dyed either. After all, God had not made sheep scarlet or purple! Many Christians in fact wore only white; they preferred the common cloak to the stylish Roman toga. Dandies came under the patristic lash. Wigs were censured, since at the laying on of hands, whose hair would the presbyter be blessing? Shaving of beards was an impious attempt to improve on the works of the Creator. As the hairs of our heads are all numbered, to pluck any out would mean spoiling God's count.

The early Christians frowned on many other things which to the modern mind are neutral. They eschewed musical instruments, gold or silver vases, white bread, foreign wines, greetings in public, warm baths and down pillows (a stone was good enough for Jacob). If this sounds naive, it was the naivety of men and women who were perhaps facing martyrdom, and who were certainly living in the light of eternity.

Amusements

We must glance finally at the early Christian's attitude to amusements. There seems to have been unanimous opposition to two leading forms of entertainment – the theatre and the gladiatorial show.

'The Devil's house' was Tertullian's name for the theatre. So all theatre-goers belonged to him. 'It is not merely by being in the world,' he wrote, 'that we fall from faith, but by touching and tainting ourselves with the world's sins. To go to the circus or theatre as a spectator is no different from sacrificing in the temple of Serapis.'

Christians had good reason for their antipathy to the theatre. There was the open display of immorality among gods and men. 'They carouse in affected manner,' wrote Tatian (c.120-173), 'going through many indecent movements; your sons and daughters behold them giving lessons in adultery on the stage.' (He might well have been writing in our day.) Christians were also unhappy about the private lives of actors and actresses. More importantly, believers might be forcibly cast in the role of criminals and executed as such on the stage. Christian 'thieves' were impaled on crosses and savaged to death by bears; others, berobed and crowned in mockery like their Lord before them, were consumed by flames.

Certainly there were plays which lampooned the faith. There is a case on record where a pagan actor, Genesius, came under conviction of sin in the course of his act. He had been parodying baptism, but he now turned to the Emperor Diocletian and confessed Christ. 'Illustrious Emperor, and all you people who have laughed loudly at this parody, believe me – Christ is the true Lord.' He was promptly tortured, but stood firm. 'There is no king except Christ, whom I have seen and worship. For Him I will die a thousand times. I am sorry for my sin, and for becoming so late a soldier of the true King.' The executioner's axe despatched him to behold the King in His beauty.

Gladiatorial combats, however, were far and away the most popular form of entertainment, attracting all strata of society from bejewelled ladies in gorgeous apparel to the impecunious slave, numbered among the 80,000 spectators who packed the Colosseum, Rome's amphitheatre.

Those facing death in the arena were regarded as the scum of the earth – criminals, barbarians, prisoners-of-war, slaves. Ten thousand such men fought in these sadistic displays during a four-month period in Trajan's reign. Some had only a net in which to ensnare fully-armoured antagonists. The pleasure-loving Emperor Commodus (180-192), self-styled 'Hercules', amused himself fighting 735 times in the arena, dressed in a lion's skin, his hair sprinkled with gold dust. For his unfortunate opponents it spelt death; he became a millionaire. Other unfortunates would be pitted against wild beasts – a lion, perhaps, or a bear. Still others were burnt alive on crosses to satisfy the blood-lust of the populace.

Clearly, no Christian could patronise such displays. Apart from the obvious cruelty, there was the problem of idolatry, since all these gladiatorial combats were dedicated to the gods. Tertullian reminded Christians that they did not eat food offered to idols. How much more should they withhold their nobler parts, their ears and eyes, from such enjoyments. 'This idolatry does not merely pass through the body, but is digested by our very souls and spirits. God has a right to claim purity here even more than in our body.' In a memorable phrase, be pictured such idolatry for the Christian as a descent 'from the sky to the sty.'

Persecution

That Christians must expect persecution in this world was made perfectly clear by our blessed Lord and Saviour Himself. 'If they have persecuted me,' He said, 'they will also persecute you' (John 15:20). And the Apostle Paul added his own testimony to the same effect: 'All that will live godly in Christ Jesus shall suffer persecution' (II Timothy 3:12).

Our purpose in this chapter is to trace the history of the persecutions of the church during the first three centuries of the Christian era. Our interest is unashamedly spiritual. The historical data provided represent the barest skeleton necessary for background and continuity.

Christians are already familiar with the persecutions recorded in the Acts of the Apostles. These were of course largely Jewish. It was in the synagogues that the apostles met the fiercest opposition to their message. Interestingly enough, it was sometimes the Roman authorities who rescued Christians from the violence of the Jewish mob. Initially, the Romans regarded Christianity as simply an offshoot of Judaism, which was a tolerated religion. It was only after the distinction became clear that the state began that series of persecutions which lasted with varying degrees of intensity down to the fourth century.

Reasons for Persecution

Before we turn our attention to the details, it will be as well to ask why men and women of eminent holiness should attract such animosity from the world. A number of reasons may be adduced for this.

In the first place, the Christian Church appeared to pose a threat to the Roman Empire herself. Unlike the Jews, a distinct nation whom the powers-that-be recognised, the church was an international organisation whose first loyalty was to Christ. 'The Jews,' wrote Celsus, 'are not to be blamed because each man ought to live according to the custom of his country, but the Christians have forsaken their national rights for the doctrine of Christ.' They were therefore seen as a subversive group, an empire within an empire, a secret society capable of disaffection and sedition.

Again, unlike Judaism, a recognised religion of respectable vintage, Christianity was new – in the words of Suetonius, 'a novel and baneful superstition.' Everyone knew that it had not received that state sanction without which it must remain illegal. Tertullian tells us that the heathen taunted Christians with the jibe: 'The law does not allow of your existence!'

The state religion itself served to accentuate the difference between 'loyal' citizens and these 'new people' called Christians. All were bound as a public duty to venerate the many gods – whose number grew with the accession of every emperor on death to the Roman pantheon. Failure to worship was construed not merely as irreligious but as unpatriotic. But how could Christians recognise Caesar as Lord? 'We give honour to Caesar as Caesar,' said one martyr, 'we offer worship to God alone.'

This refusal by Christians to worship false gods was to excite popular superstition against them. The ignorant populace construed every natural disaster as an expression of the wrath of an offended deity. Behind every epidemic, flood, drought, famine or earthquake lay the Christian refusal to give the gods their due. 'If the Tiber floods the city,' wrote Tertullian, 'or the Nile refuses to rise, or the sky withholds its rain, if there is an earthquake, famine or pestilence, at once the cry is raised: 'Christians to the lion!' ('What! All to one lion?' he added rather archly.)

The envy of pagan priests at the success of the gospel augured ill for the church. Many of these priests were also officers of state, only too ready to enlist state aid in persecution. The pattern is already clear in Acts 16, where the Philippian priests, irked at the conversion of their girl medium, charge Christians with unpatriotic tendencies and procure their punishment.

Christ had declared that He had come to cause divisions in the home –father against son and son against father; mother against daughter and daughter against mother. St. Peter speaks of the problems in the home where only one of the marriage partners is a believer. Tertullian dilates on the theme, telling of a Christian wife whose unbelieving husband keeps her from meetings, or throws dinner parties on her fast days. To the pagan living in the Roman Empire, this divisive element was a serious intrusion into the sacred realm of the family and it was not long before Christians were being accused of 'tampering with domestic relations.' Some Christians, unfortunately, added fuel to the flames by totally discounting natural ties. Lucian of Antioch, asked by his judge about his parents, replied: 'I am a Christian, and a Christian's only relations are the saints.' It was a distinction maintained right to the grave. Believing husbands would be buried with other Christians; their pagan wives would be laid in separate tombs. These domestic divisions provided subject matter for gossip and proved a further element in the growing antipathy to Christians.

The gospel call to mortification of sin and holiness of life was bound to arouse opposition. Peter tells his readers that pagans 'think it strange that ye run not with them to the same excess of riot, speaking evil of you' (I Peter 4:4). Christians were avoiding all that pagans held dear. The Epistle to Diognetus tells us that the world hates Christians 'because they set themselves against its pleasures.' Octavius complains that Christians 'abstain from the pleasures of a gentleman' – by which he meant the theatre and the gladiatorial shows! Tongues started to wag against these spoilsport upstarts who had taken it upon themselves to shun the world's pastimes. The impression of aloofness was further heightened by Christian refusal to enter professions which they considered inconsistent with their testimony.

Christians were therefore branded as antisocial – 'a people who skulk and shun the light of day, silent in public but garrulous in their holes and corners'; 'people who separate themselves from the rest of mankind.' What on earth did they do at their private meetings? Atheists they certainly were, for they had no visible gods. But why meet in secret if they had nothing to hide? Ignorant suspicion supplied the sordid answers. Had not Christ spoken of 'eating my flesh' and 'drinking my blood'? What was that if not cannibalism? Word spread that at the Lord's supper babies were sacrificed and eaten; the bread was used 'to collect the gushing blood.'

It became clear to the pagan that sex played a large part in those Christian gatherings. Christians were already known to be incestuous. Did not 'brothers' marry 'sisters'? Their meetings must be the occasion of endless sex orgies. What else could 'love feasts' connote? And why the indiscriminate 'kiss of peace'? Even Clement of Alexandria, one of their number, admitted that Christians 'do nothing but make the church resound with their kisses.' Well did Tacitus dismiss all Christians as 'a class of men loathed for their vices.'

Add to this the believer's 'arrogant' claim to salvation and his proclamation of doom against the impenitent and one can appreciate why pagan passion sometimes flared into open persecution of these 'haters of the human race'.

Nero

The man who 'first let the imperial sword rage against this sect (i.e. Christians) when it was just springing up in Rome' was the Emperor Nero (54-68). His character certainly fitted him for the role of persecutor. A debauchee of the first water, pupil of the immoral Seneca, he had his own brother, mother and wife murdered and then kicked to death his new empress, a former mistress.

The occasion for this first unsheathing of the state sword against Christians was a disastrous nine-day fire which devastated large areas of Rome in the summer of A.D.64. Rumour had it that Nero himself was the arsonist. He had sat in his country palace, lyre in hand, declaiming poems on the burning of Troy. What better background could he have desired than the Imperial City engulfed in flames?

Nero promptly deflected suspicion from himself by blaming the Christians whom he 'punished with every refinement of cruelty.' Tacitus, a violent opponent of Christianity, tells the story. Christians 'were either dressed up in the skins of beasts to perish by the worrying of dogs or else put on crosses to be set on fire and when the daylight failed, to be burnt for use as lights by night. Nero had thrown open his gardens for that spectacle and was giving a circus exhibition, mingling with the people in a jockey's dress, or driving a chariot.' Small wonder that such a sadistic wretch should recall to Christian minds the New Testament portrait of the antichrist.

Tradition has it that St. Peter suffered death under Nero. The apostle is said to have been fleeing from Rome when he met Christ. 'Where are you going, Lord?' he asked. 'To be crucified again' came the answer. Understanding this as a reference to himself, Peter re-entered the city to suffer crucifixion – upside down, at his own request, unworthy to die like his Lord.

Domitian

After a lull, a further persecution erupted under Domitian (81-96), 'the first emperor to wage a proper campaign against Christ.' He also had the dubious distinction of being the first emperor to assert his own deity. His imperial missives ran: 'Edict of the Lord our God.' Emperor and Jupiter in one, he was greeted by the crowds with cries of 'Hail to the Lord! Lord of the earth, Invincible, Glory, Holy, Lord, Blessed, Unequalled, Worthy art Thou to inherit the Kingdom. Come again. Lord for ever, Lord from eternity to eternity.' With this lunatic claim to godhead, there went sadistic cruelty and murder, which called forth Pliny's description of him as 'the beast from Hell, sitting in its den and licking blood.'

There were by now Christians in the upper strata of society and it was at these that Domitian struck. Acilius Glabrio, a consul, he forced to fight a lion and two bears – with bare fists. He then exiled him and had him executed as a conspirator.

Flavius Clemens and his wife, Flavia Domitilla – respectively the emperor's cousin and niece – ranked second in the empire only to Domitian himself. Indeed, their two sons had already been designated successors to the purple. But neither ties of blood nor status gave the emperor pause. Flavius he slew; Domitilla he banished to a small island, where for love of the Name she languished over the years in a narrow cell.

It was in Domitian's reign that the Apostle John was banished to Patmos 'for the word of God and the testimony of Jesus Christ.' Once the emperor had been despatched by an assassin's hand, John returned from exile to the oversight of the church at Ephesus.

Trajan

It was said of the Spanish emperor Trajan (98-117) that 'he would send a Christian to punishment with no more hesitation and remorse than if it had been a question of a refractory soldier or fugitive slave.' In an often-quoted letter to the emperor, Pliny the Younger, a governor of Bithynia, admits that he had promptly ordered the execution of Christians who thrice refused to deny Christ. There was no attempt to prove criminal activity. The mere profession of the Name was itself sufficient to procure death. It was I Peter 4:12-16 fulfilled to the letter. Some of those arrested did in fact recant, offering worship to Trajan and cursing Christ. And that, Pliny notes, no real Christian would ever do!

It was under Trajan that Ignatius (surnamed Theophoros), bishop of Antioch in Syria, met a martyr's death. Tradition has it that he was one of the children blessed by Christ and later sat at the feet of the Apostle John. An old martyrology records a remarkable conversation which the emperor is said to have had with Ignatius in Antioch.

'What does "Theophoros" mean?'

'One who has Christ in his breast.'

'Don't you think that gods live in us too, fighting for us against our enemies?'

'You shouldn't give the name "gods" to the demons of the nations. For there is only one God, who made heaven and earth, the sea and everything in them; and one Jesus Christ, His only begotten Son, Whose kingdom be my portion!'

'You mean His Kingdom who was crucified under Pilate?'

'His who crucified my sin with its author and has put all Satan's fraud and malice under the feet of those who carry Him in their hearts.'

'Do you then carry within you Him who was crucified?'

'I do; for it is written "I will dwell in them and walk in them".'

Trajan then commanded Ignatius to be taken to Rome and thrown to the wild beasts 'for the entertainment of the people'. On the way there Ignatius wrote: 'I long for the beasts that are prepared for me..... Now I am beginning to be a disciple. May I envy nothing of things seen or unseen that I may attain to Jesus Christ. Let there come on me fire and cross and struggles with wild beasts, cutting and tearing asunder, racking of bones, mangling of limbs, crushing of my whole body, cruel tortures of the Devil, may I but attain to Jesus Christ. I am the wheat of God and I am ground by the teeth of beasts that I may be good pure bread.' And so to the lions – and glory.

Polycarp

We now come to the classic case of Bishop Polycarp, who suffered martyrdom under Antoninus Pius (138-161). After a number of Christians from Smyrna had been cruelly tortured and thrown to the beasts, the bloodthirsty crowd called for the aged bishop. Arrested by the authorities, he remained calm in the assurance that he should suffer at the stake for the testimony of Jesus Christ. Herod, the chief of police, tried to persuade him of the harmlessness of sacrificing to Caesar as Lord. He would be safe then. But Polycarp scorned such treason. As he strode boldly into an arena filled with the cries of a blood-drunk mob, he heard a voice from heaven saying, 'Be strong, Polycarp, and play the man!'

The proconsul now urged him to think of his age. He had but to offer a pinch of incense to Caesar and say 'Away with the atheists' (i.e. the Christians). 'Away with the atheists,' Polycarp repeated, gesturing to the godless crowd. The proconsul persisted. 'Swear and I will set you free; execrate Christ.' Then came Polycarp's immortal reply: 'For eighty-six years I have been His servant, and he has never done me wrong. How can I blaspheme my King who saved me?'

The proconsul now proceeded to threaten Polycarp, first with beasts, then with fire. 'The fire you threaten,' came the reply, 'burns for a time and is soon extinguished. There is a fire you know nothing about – the fire of the judgement to come and eternal punishment, the fire reserved for the ungodly.' He then prayed with a loud voice, 'Lord God Almighty, Father of our Lord Jesus Christ, I praise Thee that Thou hast judged me worthy of this day and of this hour, to participate in the number of Thy witnesses and in the cup of Thy Christ'. And so this indomitable worthy passed through the flames to his eternal reward.

Justin Martyr tells how some were martyred in Rome simply for confessing the Name. After Urbicius, the City Prefect, had condemned a man on his confession of Christ, Lucius, a Christian bystander, protested: 'Why have you punished this man, who is neither an adulterer, a fornicator, a homicide, a thief nor a robber, and has not been found guilty of any offence but merely confesses the Name of Christ?' 'I think you are one of them yourself,' said the prefect. 'Indeed I am!' Lucius asserted, whereupon he was led away to execution, rejoicing that he was counted worthy to suffer for the Name.

Blandina

The emperor Marcus Aurelius (161-180) was a Stoic. As such, he despised Christians, dismissing Christian martyrdom as 'sheer obstinacy'. During his reign the roll of martyrs was swollen more perhaps than at any previous period.

The severest blow fell on the Christians at Vienne and Lyons in Gaul. The tide of anti-Christian fury began to swell ominously. God's people were debarred from houses, baths, the forum and even public appearance. Then some heathen domestics, fearing that they too might be subjected to the tortures Christians were undergoing, falsely accused them of cannibalism and incest. At this, the storm of pagan fury broke on the heads of these remarkable believers. Many died in prison after incredible tortures Each of them simply confessed with Blandina, a slave girl: 'I am a Christian. We do nothing to be ashamed of.'

In a lyrical passage of great beauty, the contemporary account tells us that 'the faithful were relieved of half their burden by the joy of martyrdom and hope of the promises and by love towards Christ and the Spirit of the Father. They stepped out with a happy smile, wondrous glory and grace blended on their faces, so that even their fetters hung like beautiful ornaments round them and they resembled a bride adorned with golden lace elaborately wrought; they were perfumed also with the sweet savour of Christ so that some people thought they had anointed themselves.'

'Blandina was hung in a net and exposed as food for the wild beasts let loose in the arena. She looked as if she was hanging in the form of a cross, and through her ardent prayers she stimulated great enthusiasm in those undergoing their ordeal, who in their agony saw with their outward eyes in the person of their sister the One who was crucified for them, that He might convince those who believe in Him that any man who has suffered for the glory of Christ has fellowship for ever with the living God.' As none of the beasts touched Blandina, she was returned to the gaol to await further torment.

After strengthening others in the faith and 'sending them before her in triumph to the King, blessed Blandina herself passed through all the ordeals of her children and hastened to rejoin them, rejoicing and exulting at her departure as if invited to a wedding supper, not thrown to the beasts. After the whips, after the beasts, after the griddle, she was finally dropped into a basket and thrown to a bull. Time after time the animal tossed her, but she was indifferent now to all that happened to her, because of her hope and sure hold on all that her faith meant and of her communing with Christ. Then she, too, was sacrificed, while the heathen themselves admitted that never yet had they known a woman suffer so much or so long.'

The pagans now vented their spleen on the dead bodies of the saints they had murdered. Denied burial, and exposed to wind and weather, they were now burnt to ashes and swept into the Rhone, 'in order that they may have no hope of resurrection – the belief that has led them to bring into this country a new foreign cult and treat torture with contempt, going willingly and cheerfully to their death. Now let us see if they will rise again, and if their God can help them and save them from our hands.'

What tragic blindness! These martyrs of invincible faith were already safe in the arms of Jesus, awaiting that day when God should clothe them in glorious resurrection bodies and in flaming fire take vengeance on those who know not God and who obey not the gospel of our Lord Jesus Christ.

Perpetua and Felicitas

The emperor Septimus Severus (193-211) was at first sympathetic to Christianity, but he seems to have become alarmed at the growth of the church and in A.D. 202 issued a decree forbidding Christian prose-lytism under grave penalties. Persecution broke out most severely in Egypt, where large numbers suffered for their faith. The most famous and moving story of martyrdom, however, comes from Carthage in North Africa.

The two heroines of this story are Perpetua, a lady of high station, and Felicitas, a slave girl. Perpetua herself records the pathos of her own situation. A young mother of twenty-two, she was suckling one child and expecting another. Her father, a pagan, sought to persuade her to deny Christ.

'My father,' she said, 'you see this pitcher. Can we call it by any other name than what it has?'

'No.'

'Nor can I call myself by any other name than Christian.'

'Daughter, have pity on my grey hairs. Have compassion on your father. Do not give me over to disgrace. Consider your brothers, your mother, your aunt. Consider your child, who cannot live without you. Do not destroy us all.'

Kissing her hands, he threw himself at her feet. At this she wept, knowing that he alone of all her family would not rejoice at her martyrdom. So she comforted him.

'In this trial, what God determines will take place. We are not in our own keeping, but in God's.'

So he left her, weeping bitterly. But the day of the trial saw him there again, holding up the child and saying, 'Have pity on your babe!'

Felicitas bore a child only three days before her martyrdom. When she cried in labour, the keeper of the stocks mocked her.

'Are you complaining at this? What will you do when you are exposed to the beasts?'

'It is I who suffer now, but then there will be Another with me, who will suffer for me, because I shall suffer for His sake.'

The martyrs' last meal was communal – a love feast held in public. Among the number present was the prison governor, who had by now become a Christian. Others came out of sheer curiosity. The Christians preached to them. 'Take note of our faces,' said Saturus, 'so that you may recognise us at the day of judgment.'

'When the day of victory dawned, the Christians marched in procession from the prison to the arena as if they were marching to heaven, with joyful faces, showing gladness rather than fear. Perpetua followed with radiant step as became the bride of Christ, the dear One of God.'

The heathen had hoped to persuade the Christian men to wear the robes of Saturn, the god of agriculture; for the women they intended the robes of Ceres, goddess of tillage and corn. But the Christians scorned such pagan insignia. Thus they proceeded towards the arena, 'Perpetua singing psalms, for she was now treading down the Egyptian's head.'

It was to be a fight with wild beasts. One bite from a leopard and Saturus was bathed in blood. This delighted the sadistic crowd. 'That's the bath that brings salvation,' they roared. It was a mean jibe at baptism.

Our two heroines now suffered together – Perpetua, the freeborn matron, and Felicitas, the slave-girl. It was a glorious witness to the fact that 'in Christ Jesus there is neither bond nor free.' They were hung up in nets exposed unclothed to a wild cow. The executioner, shamed at the sight, draped them with loose garments. The savage beast hurled Perpetua to the ground. She modestly adjusted her dress and her hair. Then, seeing Felicitas lying bruised, she helped her up and together they made for the gate. 'I wonder when they will expose us to the cow?' Perpetua asked. Only the sight of her bloodstained clothing and gaping wounds brought home the fact that that ordeal was already past. 'Continue firm in the faith;' she urged her brother, 'love one another, and be neither frightened nor offended at our sufferings.'

The last scene is at the heart of the amphitheatre. 'Perpetua fell into the hands of an unskilled gladiator, who pierced her between the ribs. She cried out and herself guided his trembling hand to her throat – and thus with the rest she slept in Jesus.'

The church now enjoyed her 'first long peace' – a period of affluence. Where once she had met in houses or cemeteries, she now built churches. She experienced a great access of numbers and many high-ranking court officials espoused the faith.

The peace was broken briefly with the accession of Maximin the Thracian (235-8) – a brutal eight-foot giant of massive strength and commensurate appetite. (He could break a horse's hoof with his fist – and ate forty pounds of meat a day!) He vented his spleen on church leaders in particular, as those responsible for teaching the faith which he found abhorrent. Pontianus, bishop of Rome, was exiled to Sardinia, where he was beaten to death. His successor, Anteros was also martyred after only one month in office. Many perished when the emperor purged his court of believers.

Decius

Persecution ceased with the murder of Maximin. But the clouds were gathering for the most dreadful persecution the church had yet suffered. The Goths were massing menacingly in the North, the Persians in the East. Decius (249-51), the new emperor, decided that the empire must close its ranks. There had been too many Christian conscientious objectors with their scruples about taking oaths and joining with others in pagan festivities. From now on it was to be one state, one religion. An edict of A.D.250 made sacrifice to the state gods mandatory. Only a certificate certifying that he had sacrificed could save a Christian from exile, torture or death.

The blow fell on a church which had settled on her lees and the result was utter confusion and an alarming apostasy. Many did not even make a show of resistance. In Cyprian's words, 'they fell before the fight.' He pictures them rushing to pagan altars to deny Christ and sacrifice, importuning magistrates late at night so that they might obtain the all-important certificate. They brought infants in arms with them, that they too might offer their pinch of incense to Caesar. Some of those who sacrificed were public figures, state employees perhaps. Their status, public image, profession, personal security and safety – all must come before the Christ they so readily denied.

Cyprian – who was himself later to suffer martyrdom – did not hesitate to ascribe the persecution to God's punishment of a back-slidden church. Peace had corrupted her. Many had made idols of money and possessions. They had become slaves of current fashions: 'Men wore their beards disfigured and the beauty of women was counterfeit. The eyes were changed from what God made them and a lying colour was passed upon the hair. Mixed marriages, swearing, hard words and quarrels – these and other evils troubled the Church of God. Ministers deserted their flocks in an effort to amass wealth – while the brethren were starving – and even engaged in fraud and usury.'

But the picture was not one of unrelieved gloom. Many were tortured, not accepting deliverance, that they might obtain a better resurrection. Of such were 'the unbending, blessed pillars of the Lord' in Alexandria. The aged Metras, who refused to blaspheme, and Quinta, a lady who refused to sacrifice, were tortured and finally stoned to death. Nemesion, like his Lord before him, was put to death between two thieves. Others 'were stoned, they were sawn asunder, were tempted, were slain with the sword; they wandered about in sheepskins and goatskins; being destitute, afflicted, tormented; (of whom the world was not worthy:) they wandered in deserts and in mountains and in dens and caves of the earth.' Some fell into the hands of the barbarous Saracens, who enslaved them.

Valerian

With the death of Decius at the hands of the Goths there was a brief respite. But persecution again flared under Valerian (253-8). A number of crises conspired to alarm the emperor. An epidemic ravaged parts of the empire, halving the population of Alexandria and other cities. Famine, earthquakes and tidal waves followed on the heels of searing drought and fierce tornadoes. Financial ruin came in the train of a debased currency. From east to west, heathen hordes massed on the frontiers of empire – Franks, Alemanni, Marcomanni, Persians, Goths. Valerian summoned his loyal subjects to placate the gods by sacrifice. The 'disloyal' Christians refused. Macrianus, head of the Egyptian magi, now saw his chance of revenge. Like the Philippian soothsayers before him, he hated Christians for ruining his trade by their exorcisms. A word in Valerian's ear produced the first of two edicts aimed at extirpating the church. All church leaders were to worship the state gods, on pain of exile. Christian public meetings were proscribed, as was access to the cemeteries (where most meetings were held). Large numbers of those who continued to hold meetings were arrested and either slain or condemned to the mines. But the Word of God was not bound. Those exiled to wretched outposts of empire were the means of bringing to Christ those who had hitherto lived in ignorance of the gospel.

Valerian determined on the issue of a second edict, more far-reaching than the first. Ministers of the gospel were to suffer death; senators and knights were to be demoted; ladies of the same rank were to suffer confiscation and exile; Christian employees of the imperial household or estates were to do penal servitude.

This persecution claimed some notable church leaders. Sixtus II, bishop of Rome, perished with his seven deacons; Cyprian, bishop of

Carthage, was beheaded; Fructuosus, bishop of Tarragona, was burned to death in the arena with two deacons; two Numidian bishops suffered martyrdom at Cirta. To these we must add a host of others – 'men and women, youngsters and greybeards, girls and old women, soldiers and civilians, every race and every age' who 'came through their ordeal triumphantly and received their crowns'

Valerian's end was far different. For six years the Persians paraded him in his purple robes – in chains. When he finally expired, they dyed his skin with vermilion, stuffed it with straw and hung it in a Persian temple.

Diocletian

So began the 'second long peace' for the churches, which lasted until the time of Diocletian. The number of professing Christians grew enormously; in some parts they may even have constituted a majority. Many new and large churches were erected; numbers of Christians held high office in the palace or as governors of provinces. Once more, material prosperity spawned sin and carnality – arrogance, sloth, envy, backbiting, party spirit, hypocrisy, ambition. On such a church fell the last and fiercest persecution of all.

This final persecution began at the hands of Diocletian (284-305) – a man who arrogated to himself the title 'Lord and God' and who therefore demanded the prostration before him of all lesser beings.

He was not alone, however, in his hatred of Christianity. A new form of Platonism was becoming aggressive in its opposition. Dark occult forces were also at work. Christians were blamed for bad omens during the Persian wars. The Privy Council advised persecution; the oracle of Apollo in Didyma agreed.

First to suffer were the Christians in Nicomedia, Diocletian's new capital. One day, early in 303, their great basilica was razed to the ground by the imperial troops, who destroyed all the copies of the Scriptures. The following day the first imperial edict forbade Christian meetings and ordered the destruction of churches; Bible manuscripts were to be 'handed over' for burning. Euethius, a zealous Christian, tore down the edict and ripped it to shreds, suffering death for his pains.

The new element here is the all-out attempt to extirpate the Bible.

Here was the source of Christians' strength; humanly speaking, its removal could well spell the end of Christianity itself.

There were 'traditores' who 'handed over' the scriptures to the flames. Others resorted to trickery. Bishop Mensurius of Carthage craftily secreted his valuable manuscripts and filled the empty library shelves with heretical works. These were duly burned by the unsuspecting persecutors. Felix, bishop of a village near Carthage, refused to surrender his scriptures to the flames. 'It is better,' he said, 'that I should be burned myself than the Scriptures.' The Roman proconsul in Carthage suggested that he hand over some spare or valueless books instead. But the honest bishop refused. He was taken to Italy in chains in the hold of a horse transport. And there, persisting in his 'pious obstinacy', he was beheaded for the Word of God and the testimony of Jesus Christ.

Euplius, a deacon, suffered in the same cause. Told by the judge to read the Scriptures aloud, he opened the books and read: 'Blessed are they which are persecuted for righteousness' sake: for theirs is the kingdom of heaven.' Though tortured, he repeated to the moment of death by execution: 'Thanks be to Christ, my God.'

Two fires ravaged the imperial palace at Nicomedia. Suspicion fell on Christians. Diocletian flew into a rage. Great numbers of believers now suffered torture and death – by sword, fire and drowning.

A second decree followed, ordering the imprisonment of all Christian leaders. Gaols built for homicides and criminals of all types were now flooded with Christian bishops, presbyters, deacons, readers and exorcists. Yet incarceration in these dark, airless holes on a diet of bread and water did not dampen faith. (Paul and Silas had once sung in prison. We read, too, of Pionius and his brethren, imprisoned at Smyrna during the Decian persecution, who never stopped singing 'Glory to Thee, O God!')

A third decree ordered all Christians to sacrifice, under torture if necessary, failing which they were to be put to death. It was followed by a fourth, which made the mere profession of Christianity a capital offence.

The diabolical tortures to which Christians were now subjected simply beggar description. Those descriptions attempted by some historians do not make edifying reading – floggings, grillings, exposure to wild beasts, every kind of indignity heaped on the human body.

What is edifying is the account given by Eusebius of faith standing firm under every attack: 'Nothing could be more amazing than the fearless courage of the saints under duress, the stubborn, inflexible endurance in youthful bodies. You would see a youngster not yet twenty standing without fetters, spreading out his arms in the form of a cross and with a mind unafraid and unshakable occupying himself in the most unhurried prayers; not budging in the least and not retreating an inch from the spot where he stood, though bears and panthers breathing fury and death almost touched his very flesh.'

Eusebius observed 'a most wonderful eagerness and truly divine power and enthusiasm in those who had put their trust in the power of Christ. No sooner had the first batch been sentenced than others from every side would jump on to the platform in front of the judges and proclaim themselves Christians. They paid no heed to torture in all its terrifying forms, but undaunted spoke boldly of their devotion to the God of the Universe and with joy, laughter and gaiety, received the final sentence of death; they sang and sent up hymns of thanksgiving to the God of the Universe till their very last breath.'

The persecution in the west lasted less than three years. In the east, it was more severe and continued for nearly ten years, first under Galerius (305-311), then under Maximin (305-313). In 308 the government announced more 'humane' measures. Christians were not to be slain, merely maimed! On one day alone Eusebius saw ninety-seven men, women and young children, minus right eye, left foot disabled by hot irons, making their way to the copper mines. In the same year the fifth edict reversed the 'humane' trend. Fallen idols were to be restored; all members of households (including infants at the breast) were to sacrifice; and all goods in the market place were to be polluted with libations. (No conscientious Christian would touch such goods.)

An even greater holocaust followed. The streets of some towns were strewn with Christian corpses. Day by day, believers were subjected to baiting by mobs, torture and death.

Then God's judgment fell on Galerius in the same form in which it had fallen on Herod Agrippa in Acts 12. The loathsome disease – cancer of the bowel? – induced a change of face, if not of heart. He published an edict of toleration for Christians, encouraged the rebuilding of their churches and besought their prayers for his recovery. Too late! Within a week, the emperor had gone to his account.

Unhappily, the promised peace was shortlived. After six months Maximin instituted even fiercer persecution. He established a pagan hierarchy to outshine the church; he attempted to indoctrinate children in school through the reading of the 'Acts of Pilate' – an inaccurate and slanderous account of Christ's life and death.

But the end was at hand. As delirium tremens set in, Maximin thought he saw God and white-robed martyrs coming to wreak vengeance on him. He made a last attempt to expiate his crimes by issuing an edict of toleration shortly before his death, which put an end to the persecution. The famous Edict of Milan of 313, issued by the Emperor Constantine, guaranteed complete freedom of religion to Christians. Any martyrdoms that did occur were now rare and localised.

The 'noble army, men and boys, the matron and the maid' had passed through 'the gates of pearly splendour' into the immediate presence of Him Who had Himself entered glory by His own blood. It was the unshakable certainty that He had loved them with an everlasting love and written their names indelibly on the palms of His hands which sustained the martyrs in the last frightful ordeal. When Eulalia stood trial at Merida in Spain, the judge ordered his henchmen to make furrows in her side. 'Lord,' she cried, 'they are writing that Thou art mine!' Heaven was but a step away. Hear the testimony of one for whom sudden death was sudden glory: 'Earth is shut against us,' wrote Cyprian, 'but heaven is opened; death overtakes us, but immortality follows: the earth recedes, but paradise receives. What honour, what peace, what joy, to shut our eyes on the world and men, and open them on the face of God and His Christ! Oh, short and blessed voyage!'

> 'They climbed the steep ascent of heaven,
> Through peril, toil and pain;
> O God, to us may grace be given
> To follow in their train.'

Orthodoxy and Error

The Christian Ministry

It is generally agreed that the New Testament offices of apostle, prophet and evangelist were 'extraordinary' and as such lapsed with the completion of the canon of scripture. Only two offices have survived – those of elder and deacon. The terms 'elder' ('presbyter') and 'bishop' ('overseer') are clearly synonymous and are therefore used interchangeably in the new Testament (Titus 1:5,7). Clement, writing about A.D.95, confirms this identification. The New Testament also asserts plurality of eldership in any one church and we know from early sources that this was certainly the case in the churches of Rome and Corinth (and, by implication, of Philippi).

Reference to a three-fold ministry of bishops, priests (presbyters) and deacons first occurs in A.D.115 in the works of Ignatius, bishop of Antioch. The church was under pressure. Humanly speaking, she needed strong men to maintain her unity and defend her against the inroads of heresy. In the absence of apostles, Ignatius proceeded to elevate the office of bishop above that of presbyter and give him supreme power in the local church. He told the church at Tralles 'to regard the bishop as the Lord Himself' and to obey him as she obeyed Jesus Christ.

It was the thin end of the wedge. Cyprian, bishop of carthage 249-258, compounded the error. He saw the bishop as a high priest mediating between God and His people – a sacrificing priest by divine right. He also espoused the fable of apostolic succession by which bishops claimed to trace their pedigree back to Peter, the alleged first bishop of Rome. This idea was not new, having been adopted earlier by teachers like Clement, Irenaeus and Tertullian. One difficulty was that their respective lists of bishops did not quite tally! It was all part of a process which was to culminate inexorably in the papacy and the great Roman apostasy.

The Lord's Day

It was the Apostle John who penned the first recorded reference in Christian literature to "the Lord's Day" (Revelation 1:10) – a formal designation of the church's worship day. Unlike "Sunday", the expression clearly indicates that the first day of the week is Christ's own day, "the day belonging to the Lord" and devoted to Him, as was the Lord's sabbath. "The day that the Lord hath made" (Psalm 118:24) was often interpreted by the Church Fathers to mean that the Lord Christ Himself had made the first day His own.

Some in the early church objected to the description of the first day of the week as "Sunday". That was the Day of the Sun – and they did not wish to be regarded as sun-worshippers! Other Christians, however, were content to think of the sun as a reference to Christ, "the True Light and the True Sun" (Eusebius). Christ was, indeed, "the Sun of righteousness, who should arise with healing in His wings" (Malachi 4:2). What is more, the only thing which God had done on the first day was to create light – and Sunday was the Day of Light.

This special day was a holy day, sanctified to God. Eusebius writes in the same strain when he speaks of Sundays as "holy and spiritual sabbaths". Dionysius, bishop of Corinth, records: "Today we have spent the Lord's Day as a holy day". In this, there was a parallel with the Jewish sabbath, which for Old Testament believers had been "my holy day...the holy of the Lord" (Isaiah 58:13).

If the Lord's Day was a holy day, it was also a Christian feast day, being pre-eminently the day on which the church celebrated the Resurrection of Christ from the dead. It was also the day on which their risen Lord had first appeared to His disciples. Small wonder, then, that Tertullian characterised all Lord's Days as "the festivals of the Lord". And, as festivals, these were days of great joy and gladness, "in which we rejoice and make good cheer" ("Didascalia"). "We joyfully celebrate the day on which Jesus rose from the dead", says the "Epistle of Barnabas". Chrysostom speaks of "rejoicing over ten thousand good things in the Lord's Day". There is, once again, a parallel with pre-Christian saints who had likewise found the sabbath "a delight" (Isaiah 58:13).

The Lord's Day was also a day of rest, like the Jewish sabbath, which was patently a day when all manner of work was prohibited. God had ceased from His work on the seventh day of the week, and Christians ceased from theirs on the first. Free from the demands of work and the concerns of everyday life, Christians might give themselves without distraction to what was the real object of the sabbath – the spiritual worship and service of God: "Do not make your worldly affairs of more account than the Word of God, but on the Lord's Day leave everything and run eagerly to your church, for she is your glory. Otherwise, what excuse have you, if you do not assemble on the Lord's Day to hear the word of life and be nourished with the divine food?" ("Didascalia").

Early Church Fathers make it crystal clear that it was the whole of the Lord's Day that was to be thus dedicated to God: "On the sabbath day (i.e. Sunday) all worldly pleasures ought to be abstained from. If therefore you cease from all secular works and execute nothing worldly, but give yourself up to spiritual exercises, repairing to church, attending to sacred reading and instruction, thinking of celestial things, solicitous for the future, placing the judgment to come before your eyes, not looking to things present and visible, but to those which are future and invisible, this is the observance of the Christian sabbath...He who ceases from worldly works and is free for spiritual, he it is who celebrates the sacrifice of the sabbath and the festal day of the sabbath" (Origen).

Chrysostom asserts: "Let us write it down as an unalterable law for ourselves, for our wives and for our children, to give up this one day of the week entire to the hearing and to the recollection of the things which we have heard." He pointedly contrasts the "one day" with that "small part of one day" allotted by some to public worship. And he adds a warning and an exhortation: "For we ought not, as soon as we retire from the Communion, to plunge into affairs unsuitable to the Communion, but as soon as ever we get home, to take our Bible into our hands and call our wife and children to join us in putting together what we have heard".

If further evidence were needed that orthodox Christians observed the whole Lord's Day, Tertullian also testifies to "laying aside our business on the Lord's Day". There is in addition the fact that all fasts, including those on Sundays, were in force all day long, not just for part of the day.

Many of the Fathers took delight in drawing spiritual lessons from the thought that the Lord's Day was a day of rest. They thought of it as the rest of ceasing from their own works. This had set them free to experience salvation by faith, all made possible by Christ's finished work. It was also the rest of conscience, when they ceased to do evil and began to enjoy deliverance from "sin's foul bondage". It was the rest of a holy life lived in God's Promised Land. For some, it was symbolic of the eternal sabbath of rest beyond the grave in the Glory Everlasting, when life's struggles were over.

The whole question now arises of the exact relationship between the Jewish and the Christian day of worship. We have seen that the early church drew parallels between the sabbath and the Lord's Day. Both were regarded as holy days, dedicated to the worship of God. Both were feast days, marked by great joy. Both were days of rest from secular involvement. But much more was involved than a matter of parallels. For the Fathers were fully aware that the advent of Christ had brought radical changes. Christ had fulfilled the law; the New Covenant had superseded the Old. The Fathers now noted the contrasts and their implications.

The seventh day of the week, celebrated on the sabbath, had marked the end of the old creation; the first day (the Lord's Day) had heralded the commencement of the new. Any light given on the seventh day had seemed like twilight compared with the light given on the first. The latter was the glorious light of the Resurrection of Him who was the Light of the World. "The sun has arisen," wrote one, "the lamp ceases".

Eusebius of Caesarea (c.263-c.340) is crystal clear on this. He saw the Jewish sabbath as a "shadow" of the Lord's Day. The work of the priests in the temple on the sabbath was now being fulfilled spiritually by all Christians on the Lord's Day. The old carnal sacrifices had become the Christian sacrifices of praise and joy. The sweet incense represented the prayers of the saints. The showbread and the sacrificial lamb typified the body and blood of God's Lamb, who takes away the sin of the world. "All things which it was necessary to do on the sabbath, these we have transferred to the Lord's Day, as being more closely linked to the Lord in itself and excelling, and the first and more honourable than the Jewish sabbath." Even more succinctly and unequivocally, he wrote: "The Word has exchanged and transferred the feast of the sabbath to the Lord's Day". Clement of Alexandria had said the same.

These Fathers were in fact confirming what had in practice always been the case from the very beginning. The church had always observed the Lord's Day as the "Christian sabbath". The Old Testament sabbath had now served its purpose, and had come to an end, just as the Old Covenant, of which the sabbath was the sign, had come to an end. The Lord's Day, the sign of the New Covenant, had replaced it. The "shadow" had given place to the substance.

It was a substance which maintained the essential rhythm of one day in seven stipulated in the Fourth Commandment, a holy day readily consecrated to the worship of God in Spirit and in truth. And it was a substance reflected in the other six days of the week. For, as one Father noted, Christians were "no longer observing the sabbaths, but fashioning our lives according to the Lord's Day, on which also our life arose through Him."

It is often assumed that all slaves in the Roman Empire were bound to work every day of the week, including Sunday, and were therefore debarred from attending worship on the Lord's Day. While this may well have been true in many cases, it was certainly not true of the slave in a Christian home. We know of slaves who worshipped in church on Sunday – and who did so on a spiritual equality with their freemen masters. Indeed, they might even have held office (some, for example, were deacons) while their masters were still catechumens. It is in any case true that slavery grew much less rigorous over the years, so that when, in AD321, the Emperor Constantine issued a decree declaring "the venerable day of the sun" a day of rest for all (with a few exceptions), he was simply legislating for what was already in many cases the accepted practice.

We now attempt to paint a picture of a Christian family on a typical Lord's Day in the early church. After prayer together, we see them setting out on foot from home before dawn, heading for the worship of the Lord's Day. They would be looking forward to spending the greater part of the day with the Lord's people, without the distraction of their weekday occupations. Clement of Alexandria tells us that they should "go to church decently attired, with natural step, embracing silence, possessing unfeigned love, pure in body, pure in heart, fit to pray to God". (It does sound rather like a counsel of perfection!)

The first service was normally the Communion – the Lord's Supper or Eucharist ("Thanksgiving") – which started at perhaps 7 or 8 a.m., so allowing time for those like our hypothetical family to arrive from the outlying country districts. We quote elsewhere in this work Justin Martyr's description of the Supper at Rome in his day. But practice no doubt varied somewhat from place to place and from one period to another.

At the Communion service there would certainly be readings from Scripture. Not least in view would be those Christians (perhaps many) who had no personal copy of the Scripture and others who would be illiterate. Such would be especially eager to hear God's inerrant Word read to them. One reason for the great length of these meetings would be so that worshippers might hear the whole of a Gospel (or maybe an entire Epistle) and that might well take a good hour or more. There might then be more than one exposition of given passages. Psalms would be sung – or hymns, some of which have survived. Here is one:

> *Blessed art Thou, O Lord: teach us Thy judgments.*
> *O Lord, Thou hast been a refuge to us from generation*
> *to generation.*
> *Thou, O Lord, have mercy upon us.*
> *Thou hast healed our souls in that we have sinned*
> *against Thee.*
> *O Lord, to Thee we flee for refuge.*
> *Teach us to do Thy will,*
> *Because Thou art the fountain of life.*
> *In Thy light shall we see light.*
> *Extend Thy mercy to them that know Thee.*

There would also be prayers, some of great length. In this passage from his "Apology", Tertullian – the man who said: "Prayer alone can conquer God" – explains how he prays for emperors: "For the safety of the Emperor we invoke a God who is real, a God who is living...We pray always for all emperors, that they may have a long life, a safe rule, a family free from danger, courageous armies, a faithful senate, loyal subjects, a peaceful world, all that a man and Caesar pray for."

Sunday congregations always stood for prayer. On the other days of the week, they knelt. But they stood on the Lord's Day to celebrate the Lord's glorious Resurrection. Some think that they had a further reason for standing – to celebrate their own rising from the death of sin and in joyful expectation of being raised to meet the Lord in the air at the last trump. Clearly these meetings were times of rich blessing. Origen testifies that the Lord "rained manna from heaven, the heavenly oracles" on these Lord's Days.

About midday, the gathered church would enjoy a meal together. Grace would certainly be said. The Fathers laid great stress on the necessity of consecrating every common meal by prayer. Clement actually calls every Christian meal a Eucharist.

After a siesta, some believers would take the opportunity to engage in works of mercy and necessity. With "zealous benevolence" they would visit absent church members and others to bring comfort and cheer to the disconsolate and gifts of food and other physical sustenance to the poor and needy – widows, orphans, the aged, the sick and housebound, prisoners and strangers. They knew that the Lord Himself had sanctioned such acts of kindness even on the Jewish sabbath – and Christians were enjoying much greater freedom under the New Covenant.

Later in the day, the church would sometimes enjoy a Love Feast (the Agape) of the kind narrated by Tertullian elsewhere in this account. They would then disperse in the early evening to make their separate ways home. As our family had opened the day with prayer, so the night would again find them gathered round the domestic altar before retiring to bed, perhaps about 9 p.m., unless they were able to afford lights which enabled them to go to their rest at a somewhat later hour.

Christian Worship
When the early Christians ceased to worship in either temple or synagogue, they normally did so in private homes. They were not

concerned with externals like buildings but with worshipping God in Spirit and in truth. So when Celsus (about A.D.170) taunted them with their lack of temples and images, Origen simply replied that these were unnecessary since Christians could worship their God anywhere. During troubled times, Roman Christians had perforce to worship in the catacombs. Not until about A.D.200 do we find the word 'church' used of a building.

Early church decoration was of the simplest kind, often just geometrical designs. Christians were fearful of breaking the first commandment with paintings that might attract idolatrous worship. (There are catacomb paintings, but they are almost without exception biblical. There are none at all of Christ on the cross.) It is only with the decay of primitive Christianity that we get all the gaudy decoration and paraphernalia associated with sacramentalism – gold, jewels, silk, marble, mosaics, candles and sacred vessels.

There are a number of extant records which throw light on second–century worship. Pliny the Younger, writing from Bithynia, tells us that Christians met on Sundays before sunrise to sing a hymn to Christ as God. They bound themselves by oath never to commit any crime, but to abstain from robbery, theft, adultery, never to break their word, nor to deny a trust. After that they partook of a communal meal. Justin Martyr, from Rome, explains that Christians met on Sundays because it was the first day of creation when God turned darkness to light; it was also the day of Christ's resurrection and the day when He appeared to His disciples. After Scripture reading, the president exhorted Christians to obey the word read. They rose for prayer, then partook of the Lord's Supper. Gifts were taken up for the support of widows and orphans, the sick, prisoners and strangers. (Gifts would include such things as bread, wine, olives and cheese.)

By the fourth century, church buildings had become standardised – oblong with a semicircular apse, where the bishop sat enthroned among the presbyters. Men and women gained access through separate entrances and sat apart. Small children might stand with their parents, but otherwise young and old were divided. Deacons kept order, strictly suppressing all chatter and laughter.

Cyril of Jerusalem (writing about A.D.350) tells us that services often lasted more than two hours, with readings, prayer, psalm-singing and several sermons (one by the bishop). Congregations would sometimes clap good orthodox points – an action reprehended by Chrysostom, who regarded it as much too theatrical.

The Lord's Supper

The Lord's Supper might follow an ordinary worship service or a baptismal service. After the non-Christians had withdrawn, the minister prayed, then reminded the congregation of Christ's work of redemption. He then read the words of institution and asked a blessing on the elements. After a hymn, the congregation exchanged kisses of peace, partook of the bread and wine, and sang a concluding psalm.

With time, however, sacramentalism reared its ugly head. Men became infatuated with resplendent clerical vestments and mysterious ritual. They spoke of the 'mass' and the 'altar', which was shrouded in mystery and a veil. The minister's simple dress was exchanged for the white vestment and this in turn gave way to the sacred garment of the priest.

One prayer of consecration ran: 'May God send His Holy Spirit upon this sacrifice and transform the bread into the body and the cup into the blood of His Christ.' Fears began to be expressed that impious mice might eat crumbs from the communion bread, or evil spirits lick up spilt wine and so obtain heavenly powers!

Baptism

Baptism was normally by immersion, though sprinkling and pouring were also perfectly acceptable forms. (Pictures in the catacombs depict pouring from seashells.) The Didache rightly emphasises the priority of meaning over mode. It allows all three modes and adds that the water may be cold or warm, running or static. After baptism, candidates were clothed in white robes.

Believers were at first regarded as the only fit subjects for baptism. Tertullian inveighs against the baptism of infants: 'Let them come when they are grown up; let them come when they have learned, when they are taught where they are coming; let them become Christians when they are able to know Christ.' There are no recorded cases of infant baptism in the first century. We know, however, that Origen was baptized as an infant in A.D. 185, and by the fifth century paedo-baptism had become the norm.

There was what we may call a baptismal season – from Easter to Whitsuntide. Sometimes it was restricted to one night, say Saturday to Sunday, recalling the Resurrection night, or Easter night itself.

The Book of Acts records that baptism followed immediately on profession of faith. Soon, however, it became customary to allow for a period of instruction before baptism, a period that might be as long as three years!

A catechumen had to satisfy church officers as to his motives in seeking baptism as well as his Christian character and life. Certain people (such as actors and charioteers) were ipso facto excluded. Instruction was of course given in Christian doctrine and practice, and candidates were warned against pagan practices, unclean plays, food offered to idols, necromancy, racing, gladiatorial combats and the like.

Whatever the mode of baptism employed, it was always threefold – in the Name of the Father, the Son and the Holy Spirit. Unfortunately, other elements eventually obtruded themselves – elements such as exorcism (as former pagans, candidates were demon possessed), anointing, 'sealing' with the sign of the cross and laying on of hands (when the Holy Spirit was allegedly poured out). The Didache recommended fasting – on Wednesdays and Fridays, not on Mondays and Thursdays like the hypocrites!

With the departure from biblical principles, the view gained currency that baptism washed away all previous sins. Tertullian therefore advised waiting till after marriage. The Emperor Constantine, not surprisingly, opted for a death-bed baptism.

The Love Feast
The Apostle Paul refers to the Agape or Love-feast (I Cor.11:20f.) and bemoans its abuse. Although it fell into disuse comparatively soon, Tertullian is still able to record how it was observed in its pristine purity in his day: 'Our meal shows its meaning by its name; it is called by the Greek

word for love... We do not take our places at the table until we have first taken part in prayer to God. Only so much is eaten as satisfies hunger, only so much is drunk as befits people of moderation. They satisfy their appetite like men who remember that even during the night they must worship God: they talk like men who know that their Master is listening. After water for the hands and lights have been brought in, each is invited to sing to God before the rest from what he knows of the Holy Scriptures or from his own heart... In like manner prayer closes the meal.' We may note with some trepidation that testimonies had to be sung!

Church Discipline

It is clear from a reading of the New Testament that Christians guilty of either immorality or heresy were to be disciplined. They might be barred from the communion table or even excluded from fellowship altogether. But the object of such discipline was to produce a godly sorrow and repentance leading to the restoration of the offender.

In process of time, excommunication tended to be resorted to almost exclusively for offences like adultery and fornication. Persecution then brought in its train the further problem of those who lapsed under pressure or denied the faith under torture. Opinion on the treatment of offenders varied from church to church. Rigorists like the Montanists and Novatians simply refused readmission to those whom they regarded as having committed the sin against the Holy Ghost.

Other less rigorist churches tended to establish a complicated process of restoration. We read, for example, of three classes of penitent. The 'mourners' stood outside the church in all weathers, confessing their sin and asking for prayer. The 'hearers' were in the porch with the unbelievers, listening to the Bible reading. The 'kneelers' were inside with the catechumens, but only for part of the service. Tertullian writes of the poor wretch in sackcloth and ashes, 'praying, fasting, groaning, crying out to God, prostrating himself before the elders and kneeling before other members of the congregation, as he pleads with them to carry his name before God.' The fact that Tertullian sees this 'true confession' as a 'substitute for God's wrath' which 'exchanges temporal mortification for eternal punishment' is a sad reflection on his understanding of Christian salvation.

Other Religions

Christianity was not, of course, the only faith in the ancient world which claimed man's allegiance. There were others which both made rival claims and posed a threat to the church.

Among these was Manichaeism, once embraced by Augustine of Hippo before Christ apprehended him. It was essentially eclectic – taking elements from a wide spectrum of faiths and philosophies. It taught the eternal conflict of light and darkness. God sent a succession of deliverers – Noah, Abraham, Zoroaster, Buddha and Jesus, culminating (inevitably?) in the last and greatest, Mani, the founder. Salvation was a process of deliverance from darkness, achieved by mortification of the flesh.

The Mystery Religions deserve special mention, if only because of their deceptive and seductive parallels with the Christian faith. Here were religions which spoke of the sufferings, death and resurrection of their gods.

Then there were parallels with the Lord's Supper. The initiand was invited to an elaborate sacramental meal of fish and bread. One such invitation reads: 'Chaeremon invites you to dine at the table of the Lord Serapis tomorrow, 15th, at 9 o'clock.' We recall that the great apostle had warned his readers of the table and the cup of demons (I Cor. 10:20-21).

They also boasted a counterpart to baptism. At midnight the initiand, dressed in symbolic garments, was 'buried' in a trench or grave covered with boards. A bullock or ram was then sacrificed above him so that he was 'baptised' with the sacrificial blood dripping through the holes and cracks in the boards – the blood of eternal consecration which he drank as a sacramental act. He now rose from the grave purified from sin and 'born again for eternity'. Milk was now offered to this 'twice born, new creature'. He had been through suffering and death and risen to new life with his god.

To all this we must add the many blessings held out to adherents of these mystery religions. Here were saviour gods who offered divine life, forgiveness of sins, comfort, healing, victory over demons and finally deliverance from death in the glorious resurrection at the last day, when their god would appear in judgment to summon the dead from their graves and to escort the purified soul to an eternity of ineffable bliss and glory.

Early Heresies

More serious, however, than the challenge of confessedly non-Christian religions was the hazard which arose from error in the church herself.

Already in New Testament times there were signs of departure from the faith once delivered to the saints. Some were denying the incarnation, others the resurrection. Some were legalistic, others antinomian. And there were inevitably the select few at the top – the illuminati who had greater knowledge even than the apostles themselves. Their numbers were to grow rapidly. We now glance at a few of these aberrations from the faith.

The Ebionites were legalists who sought to impose on Christians the observance of the whole Jewish law. They were in error on the person of Christ, seeing Him as divine only between His baptism and His death, which He suffered as a mere man. Their name means 'poor', and Christians were happy with it, since it indicated their essential poverty of understanding of God's law and their beggarly conceptions of Christ.

Docetists like Cerinthus, believing matter to be evil, taught that Christ had only a phantom body, so that His crucifixion was unreal. Others taught that it was really Simon of Cyrene who was crucified. Incensed at this impiety, the apostle John is said to have fled from the public baths crying: 'Let's get out of here; the place may fall in, now that Cerinthus, the enemy of the truth, is inside!'

The Gnostics were the intellectual elite who knew more than the rank-and-file Christian. Their views represented a hotch-potch of Christianity and Greek, Egyptian, Persian and Indian myths and philosophy.

Holding matter to be essentially evil, they attributed creation to an evil god, the Demiurge (the Jehovah of the Old Testament). Their supreme being, Bythos, was totally remote and unknowable. Christ, though perfect, was merely the last of a number of extraordinary 'emanations' linking Bythos with sinful man.

Men were divided into three categories – the 'pneumatic' (illuminati with superior knowledge); the 'psychic' (who merely had faith); and the 'hylic' (bondslaves of Satan and lust).

As the body was essentially evil (a Buddhist view), salvation consisted in the soul's escaping from it. This view also entailed a denial of the incarnation and of Christ's physical sufferings.

Some Gnostics (the Ophites) turned the whole Bible on its head. They regarded the serpent as the first liberator of mankind. (This presumably involved an upward fall.)

The god of the Old Testament was evil. Cain, the Sodomites, the Gomorrahites, Pharaoh and Ahab were the real saints. Moses and Elijah were the villains. Not surprisingly, Judas was reckoned the one truly enlightened apostle.

Marcion achieved notoriety by separating from the church to form a Gnostic sect. When he later approached Polycarp with the words: 'Recognise us!' he met the unexpected retort: 'I do. I recognise the firstborn of Satan!'

Rejecting the absurder elements in Gnosticism, Marcion made Scripture his basis, but foundered on the problem of evil. How could a good God create a sinful world? He therefore proceeded to drive a wedge between the two testaments. Christians had to reject the Old Testament with its cruel God of Justice. The New Testament too was pruned to square with Marcion's views. (Small wonder that Tertullian accused him of criticising with a penknife!) He argued his case in a series of antitheses. While Elisha had children torn by bears, Christ said: 'Suffer little children to come unto Me.' Whereas Paul said: 'Let not the sun go down on thy wrath,' Joshua kept the sun up till his wrath went down.

The body being the Christian's real enemy, Marcion advocated asceticism. He forbade marriage and the eating of meat. Water replaced wine at the communion table.

Such was the legalistic extreme fostered by Gnosticism. But it also fostered the opposite extreme of antinomianism. If matter was evil, there was no essential difference between lives of frugality and moral strictness and lives of licence and excess, since both were lived in the body. One group (the Encratites) actually taught that perfection is attainable only by the breach of every moral law!

Many errors arose in the early centuries regarding the nature of the godhead. Monarchians, in their anxiety to defend Christianity against the charge of worshipping three gods, fell into the error of robbing the Son either of His deity or of His personality. By suggesting that Christ was adopted as God's Son only after proving His merit, they robbed Him of His true deity. By asserting that there was only one person in the godhead, who acted now as Father, now as Son, now as Holy Spirit (like an actor with three different masks), the Sabellians robbed Him of His personality. It led to the confusion of supposing that it was the Father who was crucified.

But the attack on the person of the Son was to take a more virulent form. Arius, a presbyter from Alexandria, was driven by brutal logic to an unbiblical extreme. Since the Son could not possibly be as old as the Father, He was not eternal. He was in fact a created being and therefore different in nature and substance from the Father – neither true God nor true Man, but liable to change and even to sin.

This was clearly rank heresy, calculated to subvert the Christian faith. If Christ did not perfectly know the Father, He could not reveal Him. If He was not God, He could not offer the Father an atoning sacrifice of infinite worth.

The Orthodox Answers

What did the Church do in the face of these various attacks and aberrations? The answer is that she was driven to work out and state the biblical doctrines in precise terms and propositions. It was no longer adequate simply to confess that 'Jesus is Lord' or that 'Jesus is the Son of God'. As we have seen, there were others who were also quoting Scripture – and putting their own perverse constructions on it. Christians may have been baptised 'in the Name of the Father, and of the Son, and of the Holy Ghost.' But who were these three persons? And what was their relationship? The Sabellians had gone astray on this. Christians were going to have to hammer out a biblical theology and state it clearly in creeds and confessions of faith. And so they did!

Irenaeus (writing about A.D.180) gives us one of the earliest creeds in existence. He asserts the church's belief 'in one God, the Father Almighty, Maker of heaven and earth, and the sea, and all things that are in them; and in one Christ Jesus, the Son of God, who became incarnate for our salvation; and in the Holy Spirit, who proclaimed by the prophets the (divine) dispensations and the coming of Christ, His birth from a virgin, His passion, His rising from the dead, and the bodily resurrection into heaven of our beloved Lord Jesus Christ, and His manifestation from heaven in the glory of the Father to sum up all things in one and to raise up again all flesh of the whole human race.'

We note here that Irenaeus is consciously answering and rebutting some of the errors we have reviewed, such as the specious distinction between the God of the Old Testament and the God of the New. He is also asserting the interdependence of both testaments and the fact of Christ's virgin birth, true humanity and deity.

In a monumental five-volume work, Irenaeus slates the heretics for their arrogance. We are only finite creatures, he asserts, and must rest content with what God has been pleased to reveal in Scripture. No esoteric elite possesses further special revelation unknown to the apostles. A veil remains over problems like the origin of evil, but the Bible tells us all we need to know. It is better to walk humbly with God than to be puffed up with the 'knowledge' of Gnostic absurdities.

Tertullian's contribution was immense. He coined the term 'trinity' to express the concept of God as 'Three in One', and defined the godhead as of 'one substance in three persons'. Others, notably Hippolytus, Clement and Origen, also penned treatises.

But the threat posed by Arianism called for immediate and radical measures. Fearful of the political effects of a divided church, the Emperor Constantine called (and presided over) what proved to be the church's first ecumenical council at Nicaea in A.D.325. He did not understand the issues at stake any more than did some of the numerous bishops who attended. The debates were said to have resembled a battle in the dark, no-one knowing whether he was striking friend or foe.

Constantine, in all his regalia, may well have looked 'resplendent as one of God's angels in heaven', but God's luminary was Athanasius, a mere deacon from Alexandria without even a vote! It was his biblical insight which led the council to clarify the truth concerning God's dear Son.

To condemn Arius was an easy matter. The difficulty lay in arriving at an orthodox definition of the relationship between the Father and the Son.

It was not enough simply to quote Scripture verses, since the Arians put their own perverse constructions on them. Thus, when reminded that Christ claimed to be 'of God' or 'from God' (John 8:47), the Arians agreed, since all creation is 'of God' (I Cor.11:12). Christ was 'the power of God' (I Cor.1:24) – but so was the army of locusts (Joel 2:25). Christ was 'the image of God' (II Cor.4:4) – but so was man (Gen.1:26; I Cor.11:7). All this highlighted the urgent need to fix upon an extra-biblical term of precise denotation. This proved to be 'homoousion' – 'of one substance' with the Father.

The Creed of Nicaea therefore asserted: 'We believe .... in one Lord Jesus Christ, the Son of God, begotten of the Father, only-begotten, that is, of the substance of the Father, God of God, Light of Light, true God of true God, begotten not made, of one substance with the Father .... '

Orthodoxy had fought and won the day on the subject of Christ's deity. Battle had still to be joined on His humanity and incarnation as well as on the person of the Holy Spirit. But that is another story.

Early Schisms

At a time when Christians are having to take up definite attitudes to the ecumenical movement, a study of schisms in the early Church should prove instructive.

Some schisms arose over the problem of those who had lapsed from the faith during the persecutions of Decius, Diocletian and Galerius. Backsliders were classified under three heads: sacrificati (who had offered pagan sacrifice), thurificati (who had sprinkled incense), and libellatici (who had, by bribery, obtained certificates of sacrifice). Some Christians believed them to have been guilty of the sin against the Holy Ghost. As this was unforgivable, they were not to be readmitted to the Church. When they were readmitted, rigorists formed schismatic churches in protest against this alleged leniency.

Were the lapsed in fact guilty of the unforgivable sin? And if so, were other men in a position to know? Many argued that in persecution there were obviously attenuating circumstances, and that believers, in the weakness of the flesh, had compromised their testimony. Peter, under pressure, had once denied his Lord, and some of the lapsed had, under torture, done the same. Was that unforgivable? Dionysius of Alexandria castigated the rigorists for 'slandering our most compassionate Lord Jesus Christ as merciless.' Confessors – who had stood firm under persecution – tended to rally to the support of their weaker brethren. Unfortunately, the whole problem was bedevilled by false views of forgiveness and of episcopal power.

The Novatianists arose at the time of the Decian persecution. Styling themselves Cathari (Puritans), they unchurched all the lapsed. They also denied the validity of Catholic baptism and so rebaptised converts.

The Meletian schism occurred during the Diocletianic terror. Rigorists and laxists suffered for the faith in the same prison – divided by a curtain, since they were not on speaking terms. After release, Meletius proceeded to form 'the Church of the Martyrs' in contradistinction to 'the Catholic Church'.

We can learn more from the case of the Montanists. At first, they were anxious not to separate from the Church. But they were increasingly unhappy about the denial in practice of the priesthood of all believers. Church duties were performed by designated officials, often in a mechanical or perfunctory manner. More seriously, perhaps, the Church herself was almost indistinguishable from the world outside – not much more than a social club. The Montanists would therefore found a pure church of live saints. With such a protest against dead orthodoxy we must surely find ourselves in great sympathy.

The Montanists placed great emphasis on the Holy Spirit and His work. With that we must also surely agree. But unfortunately they went too far. Montanus taught that the Gospel Age (of the Son) had now been superseded by the New Law (the Dispensation of the Spirit). Our Lord had promised the Paraclete. That promise found its fulfilment in Montanus himself, the Spirit's mouthpiece: 'No angel, no messenger is here but I, the Lord, God the Father, have come Myself. I am the Lord God Almighty, transformed into a Man.' The ecstatic utterances of two prophetesses further compounded the error.

There followed the 'new revelations'. The Holy Spirit now withdrew 'concessions' allowed under the laxer Gospel Age. 'The flesh,' Tertullian announced, 'had had its play'. The New Law proved to be a new Legalism. Further fasts were added to those already observed by the orthodox. Virginity took pride of place over marriage (which was for the weak!). The prophetesses proceeded to abandon their husbands. Second marriage was ruled out absolutely – again, a patently antibiblical view, but Tertullian simply asserted that the Holy Spirit had now rescinded the New Testament concession.

Worse was to come. Tertullian now catalogued seven 'heinous and utterly ruinous' sins (including fornication, adultery and idolatry) which could not be forgiven. 'For these sins Christ will plead no more. These sins no man that is born of God will ever commit, and no man who has ever committed them shall be a child of God.' Thank God for First Corinthians 6:9-11!

The Montanists were commendably earnest in their expectation of the Lord's return. But here again, unfortunately, they were led astray. Priscilla, one of the prophetesses, claimed to have had a vision of the Lord at Pepuza, a village in Phrygia. He had told her that that was where the New Jerusalem would descend from heaven. Many promptly ceased work and gave away their possessions in the prospect of Christ's imminent return.

The 'prophecy' had come through a woman. Before the movement passed into history, there were to be women priests – and bishops!

The Donatist schism, which arose in North Africa during Diocletian's persecution, was the most important of the early schisms and the most long-lasting. It is particularly significant in view of the principles involved.

The immediate occasion of the schism was the action of Christians in handing over the Bible for burning by the pagan authorities. The Donatists believed fervently in the Bible as the infallible Word of God. It was their only text book (they never read pagan classical literature) and it featured prominently in their services, as did the sermon. In their desire to defend the Scriptures they asserted that anyone guilty of handing them over deserved not only excommunication but also perdition.

Like those who had separated before them, they believed the church to be an elect body of saints, separated from the world and holy. The Church of God was pure wheat from which the chaff had been winnowed. Certainly there was no place for tares. Their opponents, the 'Catholic Church' – dubbed 'the Church of Satan' by Donatists – argued that wheat and tares must remain together in the Church until the Judgment. (But surely our Lord Himself taught that the field where they grow together is not the church but the world?)

Donatists further asserted the absolute separation of Church and State. The Emperor had 'nothing to do with the church' and should not presume to lecture her. (God had given prophets – not kings – to teach Israel.) The Catholics were the real schismatics – the traitorous 'Church of Judas' who joined hands with an impious state to persecute God's people So be it! That was God's way of separating the just from the unjust.

Augustine, unfortunately, encouraged the persecution. The emperor was 'God's avenger' to deal with Donatist 'heretics' and 'criminals'. He could use the secular power to 'compel them to come in' and thus escape eternal punishment.

The Donatist bishops did not lord it over God's heritage. Other church officers were 'fellow-presbyters who have been appointed with us ministers in the Gospel'. Church members were 'the people who share our warfare in the truth of the Gospel'.

Inevitably, differences between Donatist and Catholic were not solely spiritual. They differed in language (Berber or Punic as against Latin); in culture (local against classical); in politics (colonised against imperialist); in economics (poor farmers against wealthy landowners maintaining the 'divinely-ordained' status quo).

It was a sad story of intrigue, fanaticism and violence on both sides. Murderous bands brandishing clubs, screaming 'Praises to God!' and hurling themselves over precipices or into the fire do not strike one as Christian martyrs.

Though the Catholics enlisted the armed might of imperial Rome against them, the Donatists survived the vicious onslaught and were still in North Africa in the seventh century when the hordes of Islam swept all before them.

It is all too easy to focus attention on the immediate occasion of the various schisms – the unforgivable sin, charismatic gifts, the validity of orders and the like. The real question we have to face is: What is the Church? If she is the mixed multitude of 'Catholic' theology, then the schismatics were guilty of sinfully dividing the body. If on the other hand she is Christ's bride, then the schismatics did right to call her out from among the unregenerate. It is hardly an academic question for twentieth-century Christians.

Early Apologies

During the early centuries of the Christian era many written attacks were launched against the faith once delivered to the saints. Some of them have a very modern ring! We here review some of the charges made and some answers proposed by Christian apologists.

The Bible itself came under fire as unreliable, unhistorical, unscientific and full of contradictions and myths. The God of the Bible was charged with being subject to human passions like anger and fickleness. Why did He create horrible creatures like snakes? Why did He allow sin and suffering? And He was so weak – too weak to save Jesus and the martyrs from death.

If God really did come down in the Incarnation, why did He come? Not to find out the facts, surely? Wasn't He omniscient? And if He knew of man's plight, why didn't He come sooner? Perhaps He didn't care? The Incarnation was in fact a hoax. Jesus was Mary's illegitimate son. He turned magician and promptly claimed to be God. But whoever heard of God being born? Or eating? Or fearing? Or dying on a cross? How despicable! The disciples – crafty rogues – fabricated the myth of Jesus' resurrection. Only one person saw Him risen – a neurotic woman! Why didn't He appear to prominent unbelievers?

Christians next came under the lash. They were the scum of society – slaves, women and little children, who were not only ignorant and illiterate but positively obscurantist. Yet they had the effrontery to describe the talk of the great philosophers as 'empty chatter'! Christian 'atheism' had provoked the gods into sending down droughts, earthquakes, famines and pestilences. To the lion with them! Christians rejected emperor worship. How disloyal! Their religion was universal, embracing Europeans, Asians and Africans. How unpatriotic! They rejected both political office and military service. How antisocial! If everyone behaved like that, the empire would be overrun by barbarians. Yet Christians claimed all the civic privileges (like freedom and marriage). The best place for them was the desert – or the grave! For good weight, they were also charged with infanticide, cannibalism and incest.

Most of the charges were answered by the Christian apologists – with varying degrees of success. Origen was weak in his defence of Old Testament historicity. Here he simply took refuge in allegorisation. He did better in his defence of Christ and the apostles. Christ's massive influence on history proved His deity. Though a poor uneducated labourer from a remote village, He had overthrown paganism, won converts (including the learned!) and shaken the whole world more than any philosopher, emperor or general! The disciples were not rogues. You don't risk your life for a hoax. Their boldness was proof positive of the resurrection. They were honest men, who recorded sins like Peter's denial and their desertion of Christ.

Christians were not arrogant in claiming to know better than the philosophers. They had abandoned the heroic 'search' for God and simply submitted to His revelation.

Justin replied to the charge of atheism by asserting that Christians worshipped the one true God. The other gods were, quite simply, demons. Many apologists poured ridicule on the pagan deities. They were the vanities of Psalm 115 – bits of wood, stone or metal that decayed before your very eyes. Dumb, blind and lifeless, they had to be protected against theft! Tertullian reminded pagans that they themselves mocked their own gods on the stage and sold them – or melted them down to make saucepans! Were Christians really being asked to worship the classical gods – corruptible matter thrown up by sea or land? Or trees and rivers, cats and mice, snakes, crocodiles and dragons? Pagans had a goddess for bees. Why not have one for beets, cabbages, cress, figs and marrows? The gods were just like human beings. They got angry, fell in love, committed adultery, stole, murdered – and finally died. And how ugly they were! Some had a hundred hands; Hercules was a dragon; Jupiter's daughter had four eyes, horns and an animal face on her neck.

Tertullian asserted that, far from being Christians, it was pagans who brought calamities like earthquakes. Christians tempered the world's evil, and by prayer and fasting produced rain for all. He vigorously defended believers against the charge of social irresponsibility. Christians were in fact the best citizens. They prayed for the Emperor and for peace – unlike the pagans, who mouthed formal prayers, and then planned subversion! They played a full part in society. All they avoided was sin – like sharp practice in business.

The Epistle to Diognetus presented a moving picture of the Christian life. Christians were no different from others in country, language, custom, food or dress. They weren't segregated in Christian towns with their own speech and life-style. But though in the flesh, they did not live after the flesh. Good citizens on earth, their real citizenship was in heaven. In the world, they were not of it, for they were strangers and pilgrims here. Loving all, they were persecuted by all. Put to death, they rose to life. Paupers themselves, they made many rich. Lacking everything, they abounded. Dishonoured, they were glorified. Being reviled, they blessed. Doing good, they suffered as evildoers. Persecuted, they rejoiced. As the soul preserves the body, Christians preserved the world. Living in a corrupt world, they awaited incorruptibility in heaven.

Tertullian answered the charge of atrocities. Infanticide? Christians did not even procure abortions – the premature murder practised by pagans. It was pagans who murdered infants by drowning or exposure to cold, starvation and wild beasts. Cannibalism? Christians would not even eat sausages containing animal blood. No! Christians were holy people. Meetings were not for crime but for prayer, Bible reading and exhortation. Unlike pagans, Christians did not spend their money on banquets and drinking parties. It went to the poor, orphans and prisoners. Meetings began and ended with prayer, when the Christians dispersed quietly. The pagans were the hooligans and criminals. There were Christians in prison – but only for being Christians!

Other apologists emphasised the transforming power of Christ in the life. He made men meek, loving and kind. The fornicator became pure; the erstwhile dabbler in the occult now worshipped the true God; the avaricious gave to others; malicious murderers lived in peace and prayed for their enemies. When struck, they did not strike back; when robbed, they did not go to law. They gave to those who asked of them, and they loved their neighbours as themselves.

Early Monasticism

Monasticism is clearly not a New Testament ideal. Our Lord explicitly warns His people against the error of segregating themselves from society in a vain attempt to demonstrate that they are 'not of the world' (John 17:14,15) The Apostle Paul makes the point that if we wished to have no contact at all with unbelievers, then we should have to leave the world altogether (I Cor. 5:9,10).

History itself confirms that monasticism is certainly not 'Christian' in origin. We read of ascetics in the second century B.C. who walled themselves up in the temple of Serapis at Memphis. There were Jewish quietists who took up residence in caves during the Maccabean wars. The better-known Qumran Essenes and the Therapeutae must also rank as early monks who were patently not Christian.

The question therefore arises as to why Christians ever came to abandon the world and seek refuge either as hermits or in isolated communities. There are a number of answers to this question, the first of which may surprise us – and should evoke our sympathy, if not our approval. It is that true believers were thereby registering a protest against the influx of pagans into the church. When it became socially expedient to become a church member, and any Tom, Dick or Harry could do so, it was time for the saints to leave. It is a simple fact of history that the first Christian anchorite was a Novatianist – a member of a rigorist sect which emphasised the purity of the gathered church.

Other (less respectable) motives lay behind the monastic movement.

It was argued that sin was a social phenomenon and therefore the obvious solution was to drop out of society and live alone. (The earliest Christian monks were anchoritic.) This surely argues a pitiful ignorance of the nature of sin as 'the plague of the heart'. It was something the hermits were to learn to their cost. Jerome's flight from society did not banish visions of Rome's dancing girls. Not could they be expelled by beating the breast with rocks!

A further motive was the desire to emulate the martyrs who had sealed their testimony with their blood. If there were no longer persecutors or beasts to fight in the arena, then they would become 'martyrs in intention', fighting against the demons they imagined to inhabit the desert wastes.

One must also mention the economic motive. Some entered monasteries for the board and lodging offered in return for labour. Others sought relief from crippling taxation!

Eusebius tells us that the first Christian hermits were refugees from the Decian persecution, but Antony (251-356) is credited with founding the anchorite movement proper. He abandoned a life of luxury for the rigours of desert life. Here he practised that asceticism which was regarded by many as the hallmark of the true Christian, 'the whole yoke of the Lord'. Shut up in a tomb, then in an old fort, and finally in total isolation on a mountain, he thought to fight Satan and his host with the mere sign of the Cross.

Antony's story is the depressingly familiar one of endless visions and miracles. Wild animals, we are assured, obeyed and served him. In spite of his memorisation of Bible texts, Antony appears to have remained ignorant of Bible truth. He believed in man's essential goodness and taught a 'gospel' of salvation by works.

Pachomius (290-345), the founder of the Monastic movement, and Basil (329-379) must at least be given credit for realising that the solitary life of the hermit is basically misconceived. Basil, in arguing his case for communal as against solitary living, adduces points with which we must surely find ourselves in agreement. First, he argues that since we are interdependent, our physical needs are more easily met in communities. Secondly, communal living is a check on selfishness. Man is a social, not a solitary being. 'Whose feet will you wash?' he asks the hermit. 'Whom will you serve? How can you be last of all if you are alone?' (His case is unanswerable.) He follows up his advantage by indicating in the thiird place that hermits have no-one to point out their faults and so they become self-satisfied – something that is very difficult when there are others round to administer rebukes! Fourthly, he shows that only communities are able to fulfil certain biblical injunctions, like giving food, clothing and medicine to the needy. Finally, he asks how a hermit can possibly display humility, compassion or patience!

From a biblical viewpoint, the start of the monastic movement was hardly auspicious. A 'revelation' was given – in a form with which we have become familiar. An angel appeared to Pachomius in a cave and commissioned him to found an order of monks. The rules of the order were engraved on a brass tablet, which the angel presented to him. (The Mormons went one better. They received gold tablets. But that, of course, may have been to signify that their destiny was to be not poverty but wealth.) The Pachomian rules, mostly rather trite, contain some bizarre elements. The monks' faces were to be veiled at table to prevent recognition – and conversation. The ascetic element comes out in the requirement that monks should sleep on sloping seats!

Pachomius duly proceeded to establish organised communities on the basis of these rules. They were self-supporting settlements, each inmate plying some kind of trade, such as mat-weaving, shoe-making and tailoring. In fairness, it should be said that the Bible was the basis of instruction in the monasteries. The monks memorised whole passages of Scripture, notably psalms or epistles. There were no ascetic extremes. An offender might, for example, forgo a meal or be put on bread and water for a while. Needless to say, a great wall shut them off from the outside world.

Basil extended the whole concept of monastic life. Monks now aimed to serve the community at large, rather than their own narrow interests. Many of them ran schools and hospitals.

Both hermits and monks in monasteries adopted that false view of mortification known as asceticism. It was based on the old Dualistic heresy which regarded matter (and therefore the body) as inherently evil. This led men to abuse their bodies physically in a vain attempt to subdue sin.

Some aspects of asceticism were comparatively mild, such as wearing a hair shirt, going barefoot, sleeping on the ground and abstaining from wine. Inevitably, however, there were the excesses which revolt the enlightened Christian mind.

Macarius of Alexandria, who lived on cabbage leaves and stood upright for the whole of Lent, was relatively moderate. We read of hermits living in cisterns, wearing iron belts and collars and bound in chains so heavy that they could only walk bent. One monk, Baratos, at first walled up, betook himself to a lath crate, which was exposed to the elements and so small that he had to crouch. Another, Thelalaios, lived in a tiny cylinder suspended in mid-air, his thighs flexed against his trunk. Pachomius entered a hyenas' cave in the hope that they would devour his sinful flesh. They did not oblige.

The case of Symeon Stylites (c.389-458) is notorious. Already in his teens he was wearing a tight cord which drew blood. After being successively 'buried', walled up and chained, he then determined to take refuge up increasingly higher pillars till he finally mounted one seventy feet in height with a platform four square yards in area There he remained until his death thirty years later. Sightseers came from as far afield as Britain. He spent his time in continuous 'prayer', dropping rhythmically to his knees and touching the platform with his forehead. Theodoret counted 1,244 obeisances before giving up. It is said of this poor benighted zealot that when he failed to escape from society horizontally, he decided to do so vertically!

It is clear from this case that prayer very easily degenerated into meaningless forms. It was, in any case, never extempore. The monks used the Lord's Prayer and set prayers. Paul of Scete memorised 300 prayers, which he recited daily, dropping a small pebble for each. He became very depressed when he heard of a woman who could recite 700! Lucius of Enaton used to recite Psalm 51:1 continuously at work. Can that have been anything other than vain repetition?

Not surprisingly, public worship tended to become liturgical and mechanical. Alexander founded a monastic group known as Acoimetai (the Unsleeping Ones), who were to reflect on earth the ceaseless praise of angels in heaven. So every three minutes of day and night monks would fall on their knees as they sang 'Glory to God in the highest and on earth peace, goodwill towards men'. It was a paean of praise destined to last for centuries. A noble concept, no doubt, but was it Christian?

What of the Scriptures? Here again, unfortunately, we have the same mechanical approach. Though monks memorised passages – indeed, some of them learned the whole Bible by heart – it seems to have had no effect on their understanding of the Christian life. More reliance was placed on the so-called 'Sayings of the Fathers', an anthology of utterances by venerable monks which were regarded as inspired. Amoun is actually on record as saying: 'It is preferable to use the Sayings of the Fathers and not passages from the Bible; it is very dangerous to quote the Bible'! Small wonder, then, if they followed cunningly devised fables. Small wonder, too, if they laid claim to all manner of visions – visions of Mary, of angelic choirs, even of God Himself.

Miracles also abounded. The blind, the lame, the demon-possessed – all were cured. (Healings are no modern phenomenon.) Animals ran errands or stood guard, as required; they obligingly avoided treading on newly planted herbs. A 'holy' monk could, at a word, kill an enemy or produce an earthquake. We are assured that one such monk walked on water, flew through the air and halted the setting sun till he had reached his destination. After such feats, it was child's play to rivet an enemy to the spot with a word, or prevent stolen cabbage from boiling.

Monks pictured themselves as 'athletes' engaging in battle with demons in the desert places. Their weapons were asceticism, prayer and Bible texts, which they hurled at the Devil. The 'demons' they assailed were thought of in terms of certain sins, notably adultery, arrogance, avarice, despondency, gluttony, irritability, sloth and weariness of being a monk. These were, admittedly, sins – with the obvious exception of the last. But asceticism, prayer by rote and mechanical repetition of Scripture were scarcely calculated to win the victory. Poor souls! They had no real knowledge of Biblical truth. (The Egyptian monks rarely even mentioned the name of Jesus!) For them, the glorious Cross on Calvary's hill was nothing but a sign to scare off demons.

One has more than a shrewd suspicion that what motivated many monks was a pathological fear of sex. They gave celibacy pride of place. Some even thought that the married would be excluded from heaven! Women represented a perennial danger – 'the instrument of Satan', in fact. Monks never looked at them. There is a pathetic story of one monk who turned aside when he saw nuns approaching. A battle-axe of an abbess reprimanded him with the words, 'If you had been a perfect monk, you wouldn't have looked closely enough to know that we were women!' 'Is the desert the only place where there are no women?' asked Abba Sisois. 'Take me to the desert!'

Apocryphal Writings

With the monks, we are in the world of the Apocrypha, and to that we now turn.

At a time when the New Testament canon had not been universally agreed, a great number of uninspired writings made their appearance, each laying claim to canonicity. They usually enhanced their pretensions by styling themselves 'Gospels', 'Acts', 'Epistles', or 'Apocalypses'.

The instructed Christian will at once discern their spurious character. We find ascetic elements, like the premium placed on continence. There are also Gnostic and Docetic elements, with their denial of the person and work of Christ, together with much that the Christian will find repulsive.

As might be expected, the miraculous element looms large. Our Lord is represented in His infancy, making clay sparrows that could fly, stretching planks to the right length, producing clothes of different colours from black dye, turning goats back into children, and sliding safely down a sunbeam. He is blasphemously reported as killing others in anger and then restoring them to life.

The Apostle John swims to Ephesus – on a cork. He escapes unscathed from a cauldron of boiling oil. Bugs which he turns out of his bed wait patiently till allowed back to their cracks the next morning. Peter, among other things, makes a dried sardine swim and repairs a broken statue by sprinkling water on it.

The 'Acts of Paul' boasts a plethora of incredible myths, like that of the baptised lion. (The mode of baptism is not specified, but the thought that it might have been immersion makes the mind boggle.) It contains the now celebrated description of the great Apostle as 'a little man, going bald, with crooked legs, a strong body, eyebrows joining and a rather aquiline nose; full of grace, for at times he looked like a man, and at times he had the face of an angel.'

The 'Acts of Thomas' seems to major in asses. One of them traces its pedigree from Balaam's ass through that ridden by our Lord. Another, not to be outdone, exorcises demons, exhorts Thomas to perform miracles, and preaches to the people. We are not therefore surprised to learn that one dream narrated is an exact reproduction of an Indian myth.

No-one would object to the picture painted of heaven – a glorious place full of light, blossoms, fruit and sweet perfumes. The picture of hell, however, is little short of revolting. Some of the milder statements reveal blasphemers hanging by their tongues; adulterers with their heads in mire; abortionists up to their necks in lakes; false witnesses with flaming fire in their mouths; late risers on Sunday in a cloud of fire; murderers tormented by creeping things. One need hardly add that all this is very far removed from the New Testament picture.

We turn from the unedifying musings of sick minds to the glorious truth of God's Word. We leave the make-believe world of the monks and the Apocrypha for the real world of those who 'through faith subdued kingdoms, wrought righteousness, obtained promises, stopped the mouths of lions, quenched the violence of fire, escaped the edge of the sword, out of weakness were made strong, waxed valiant in fight, turned to flight the armies of the aliens.'

Surrounded as we are by 'so great a cloud of witnesses, let us lay aside every weight and the sin which doth so easily beset us, and let us run with patience the race that is set before us, looking unto Jesus the author and finisher of our faith; who for the joy that was set before him endured the cross, despising the shame, and is set down at the right hand of the throne of God.'

Bibliography

ALEXANDER, D. & P., ed. Lion History of Christianity. Lion Publishing (1977) 656pp.

ATKINSON, B. Valiant in Fight. Inter-Varsity Fellowship (1950) 192pp.

BECKWITH, R.T. & SCOTT, W. This is the Day: The Biblical Doctrine of the Christian Sunday. Marshall, Morgan & Scott (1978) 181pp.

BETTENSON, H., ed. & tr. The Early Christian Fathers: A selection from the Writings of the Fathers from Clement of Rome to Athanasius. Oxford University Press (1956) 424pp.

BROADBENT, E.H. The Pilgrim Church. Pickering (1931) 406pp.

BRUCE, F.F. The Growing Day (to AD 313). Paternoster (1951) 192pp.

CHADWICK, H. The Early Church. Penguin (1967) 304pp.

DAVIES, J.G. The Early Christian Church: A History of its First Five Centuries. Baker (1987) 314pp.

DE PRESSENSE, E. The Early Years of Christianity: A Comprehensive History of the First Three Centuries of the Christian Church. Hodder & Stoughton (1879) 4 vols., 2194pp.

DUCHESNE, L. Early History of the Christian Church: From its Foundation to the End of the Fifth Century. John Murray: London (1909-1924) 3 vols., 1527pp.

FERGUSON, E., ed. Encyclopedia of Early Christianity. Eerdman (1955).

FISHER, G.P. History of the Christian Church. Hodder & Stoughton (1913) 729pp.

FOAKES JACKSON, F.J. History of the Christian Church to A.D. 461. Hall (1905) 535pp.

GWATKIN, H.M. Early Church History to A.D. 313. Macmillan (1909) 2 vols., 686pp.

HOUGHTON, S.M. Sketches from Church History. Banner of Truth (1980) 255pp.

KIDD, B.J. A History of the Church to A.D. 461. Oxford University Press (1922) 3 vols., 1477pp.

LATOURETTE, K.S. A History of the Expansion of Christianity. Zondervan (1976) Vol.1, 402pp.

LIETZMANN, H. The Beginnings of the Christian Church. Lutterworth (1962) 303pp

MILLER, A. Miller's Church History.
Pickering (1900) 3 vols., 1091pp.

OETTING, W. The Church of the
Catacombs. Concordia (1964) 131pp.

RENWICK, A.M. The Story of the Church.
Inter-Varsity Fellowship (1958)
222pp.

SCHAFF, P. The History of the Christian
Church to A.D. 311. T. & T. Clark
(1869) 535pp.

SCHAFF, P. History of the Christian Church:
Ante-Nicene Christianity.
T. & T. Clark (1889) 2 vols., 868pp

SMITH, M.A. From Christ to Constantine.
Inter-Varsity Press (1971) 208pp.

WAND, J.W.C. A History of the Early
Church to A.D. 500. Methuen (1953)
290pp.

WILLIAMSON, G.A., tr. Eusebius'
Ecclesiastical History. Penguin (1994).

WORKMAN, H.B. Persecution in the Early
Church: A Chapter in the History
of Renunciation. Charles H. Kelly: London
(1906).

Other books from Day One

The Beatitudes for today

John Blanchard

Large format paperback
263 pages   **£7.95**

In his foreword, Eric J. Alexander points out that "this book fills a significant gap in contemporary Christian writing. Although the past thirty years have seen the publication of several excellent volumes on the Sermon on the Mount, we have lacked a full-length treatment of the Beatitudes. The Christian world has been deeply indebted to John Blanchard for his preaching and writing ministry over many years. Both are characterised by an absolute faithfulness to the text of Scripture, a deep concern to apply God's Word to today's world, and a God-given insight into the implications of biblical truth."

John Blanchard is an internationally known British Evangelist and Bible teacher, who has written a number of best-selling books including *Ultimate Questions, Right with God, Pop Goes the Gospel* and *Whatever Happened to Hell?*

ISBN 0 902548 67 0

The Lord's Prayer for today

Derek Prime

Large format paperback
163 pages   **£5.95**

The Lord's Prayer is the only pattern prayer the Lord Jesus provided and is timeless in purpose and function. It indicates how we are to pray throughout our life in this present world. Its truths do not change. It is essential for us us to be reminded of them.
The Lord's Prayer reminds us, at its very beginning, that true worship of God arises from a living relationship with Him as our Father through our Lord Jesus Christ.

Derek Prime was for many years the pastor of Charlotte Baptist Chapel, Edinburgh. He is now a well-known convention speaker and author of many books including *Let's Say The Grace Together* and *Gofors and Grumps.*

ISBN 0 902548 68 9

For further information about other Day One titles, call or write to us:

0181 313 0456
IN THE UK

In Europe: ++ 44 181 313 0456
In North America: 011 44 181 313 0456

Day One Publications 6 Sherman Road, Bromley Kent BR1 3JH England